Will You Love Me?

Also by BARBY KEEL

Gabby: The Little Dog Who Had to Learn to Bark

Will You Love Me?

THE RESCUE DOG THAT RESCUED ME

BARBY KEEL

with Cathryn Kemp

CITADEL PRESS
Kensington Publishing Corp.
www.kensingtonbooks.com

CITADEL PRESS BOOKS are published by

Kensington Publishing Corp.
119 West 40th Street
New York, NY 10018

First published by Trapeze, an imprint of the Orion Publishing Group Ltd, an Hachette UK company.

All Kensington titles, imprints, and distributed lines are available at special quantity discounts for bulk purchases for sales promotions, premiums, fund-raising, educational, or institutional use. Special book excerpts or customized printings can also be created to fit specific needs. For details, write or phone the office of the Kensington sales manager: Kensington Publishing Corp., 119 West 40th Street, New York, NY 10018, attn: Sales Department; phone 1-800-221-2647.

ISBN-13: 978-0-8065-4061-0
ISBN-10: 0-8065-4061-3

First trade paperback printing: October 2020

10 9 8 7 6 5 4 3 2 1

Printed in the United States of America

Electronic edition:

ISBN-13: 978-0-8065-4062-7 (e-book)
ISBN-10: 0-8065-4062-1 (e-book)

CONTENTS

INTRODUCTION

Pipzedene occupies twelve acres of lush, rolling Sussex countryside off Freezeland Lane in Bexhill. I bought the land in 1971 with savings I'd scraped together through working as a chambermaid for ten years, and with help from my partner at the time, Les, although the majority of it was paid for by me.

I'd always dreamt of owning land. I've never cared about houses or possessions, and ever since I was a little girl all I had wanted to do was look after animals, and someday provide them with a safe home to live out their lives in peace and harmony.

On a spring day in 1971, I stepped out of the car and took in the sight of the swathes of vivid green fresh grass and trees bursting into life after their winter slumber. I knew I'd arrived somewhere special. I breathed in the scent of flowers and woodland, of mud and pasture, and I knew in my bones that this land was meant to be mine. I bought it that day, and within a couple of weeks I had moved myself, Les, a devilishly handsome man with golden hair and a charming smile, and my aging father, who was in his late sixties, onto the site in

1

two dilapidated trailers. My two dogs, a spaniel called Pip and a German shepherd called Zede, bounded out of the back of the car and tore into the paddock, barking and leaping with joyful abandon. The sight of their glee at seeing all the space to play in and the smells to swoon over made my heart sing. At that moment I knew I was home.

The original plan was to settle there and to take in a few stray animals. When I was a child, my father had rescued many a beleaguered stray or pet shop animal by bringing them home to be cared for, and it was something my father and I shared together. I would often race home from school and wait by the front gate to see if Dad was coming back with a new pet, usually a bedraggled-looking cat or dog, though once it was a monkey and once even a bush baby. He spent most of the little money he earned as a chef in a small hotel in Eastbourne on giving these creatures the life they deserved.

My father had a gentle presence, a sweet nature, and a glint in his eyes. He'd peer over his spectacles while checking over each new find, before reassuring himself that all the animal needed was a bit of love and tenderness. He gave that in spades, and I'm sure that his love for those animals was the catalyst for my lifelong passion for furry, feathery, or scaly friends.

Looking after these charges was the way my dad and I spent time together, and I adored our shared evenings, trying to coax a kitten into eating some leftover meat or bread soaked in milk. In those days, we had little enough to share, and I marveled at my dad's courage in risking the wrath of my mother in bringing home yet another hungry mouth, albeit a furry one, to feed. My mum would stand in the doorway, her bulky frame simmering with resentment, her hands on her hips, shaking her head slightly. He would come in, a dog trotting after him or a cat in his arms, and he'd smile as if she was thrilled to see him. That used to make me chuckle, and anyone who dared defy my rather overbearing mother was a hero to me.

Dad waited until he and Mum had separated before he dared bring home the monkey, though. By then he was living with me, a girl in her twenties, in a ground-floor apartment. Seeing that daft creature, I was wary at first, but I couldn't help bursting out laughing.

"Dad, what have you done this time?" I shrieked, as the monkey jumped onto my shoulder and began scratching softly at my ear. "He looked miserable in that shop. . . . I just had to buy him," Dad replied, shrugging his shoulders and making me laugh again at the incongruous nature of our life. Before I'd even put the kettle on to make tea for him, he'd walked out to the shed and started gathering materials to build the monkey its own cage, taking up half the tiny living room in the process. I didn't mind. I was as besotted as Dad was.

Taking in animals was as natural to me as breathing country air, and it wasn't long after I'd bought the land, which I named Pipzedene after my three animals—Pip, Zede and my bush baby Deana—that people started bringing strays to me. I started by providing refuge for a few dogs and a couple of cats that roamed free across the land, then came the horses, then chickens, then a sheep or two. Once the larger animals arrived, I set about putting up fencing around the boundary of my land. I wanted the animals to live freely, but didn't want them running across or up the lane and causing havoc for my neighbors.

I had to sell my car and stop my life insurance to pay for the wood, but I didn't care. Who would I leave my land to anyway? I had never wanted children, and none ever came. My animals have always been my babies. I have fed, nursed, cuddled, and shared my home with hundreds, perhaps thousands, of animals that have needed my care over the past thirty-seven years.

The trickle of strays and abandoned mutts and cats soon became a deluge. I needed to build more enclosures: pens for the cats, kennels with runs for the dogs and spaces for the rabbits, chickens, cockerels, geese, ferrets, sheep, cows, goats, horses, and pigs, which I did brick by brick so that they could live out their lives here. Les and I built a bungalow for us, but, unbeknownst to me, he didn't apply for planning permission, and council planners forced us to knock it all down only months later. We lived in a leaky old trailer, then when our relationship ended and Les moved out, I stayed there alone for almost twenty years before saving enough money to build another home, a small, squat single-story building that sits in the heart of the land.

In 2002, when we became a registered charity, Pipzedene became the official site of the Barby Keel Animal Sanctuary, and it is here, in this special place, that I have dealt with the daily arrival of unwanted, abandoned, hungry, and neglected animals that find their way to me. For many, we are their last hope. All of my animals have a sad story to tell. Some have suffered at the hands of their previous owners. Others have been neglected and left to fend for themselves, almost starving in the process. Many have suffered through sheer indifference. Some healthy young animals have missed death by a whisker, having been taken to a vet or animal center to be put down because the owner no longer wanted them. It is astonishing and heartrending, and every day I shake my head at the cruelty and selfishness of fellow humans. Yet every day, my volunteers here at the sanctuary show me otherwise, that they can dedicate their lives to giving comfort and hope to animals who may have been destroyed or dumped if we weren't here.

All the animals that come to the sanctuary are fed and given a warm bed and medical treatment, if required. Those who are too old and infirm to be rehomed will remain at the sanctuary to live out their lives, while the enormous task of finding homes for the others is an ever-present worry. I always joke I am a matchmaker between animals and people, but it is a job I take extremely seriously. No animal can leave without me knowing for sure they are going to a loving, permanent home. I am fierce like that. My staff tell me I have a black belt in "gob" and they're right. When it comes to creatures, I'm never afraid to open my mouth in my efforts to protect them.

For the first few years, my dad and I did everything, until he passed away. Even though I'm in my element hefting great bales of straw or digging out a hole to stake out a fence, I knew I needed help. Little by little over the weeks, months, and years, my reputation grew through word of mouth. People started coming and asking if they could volunteer, and over time I had my "motley crew," the band of animal lovers who, like me, only wanted to help their fellow creatures. Their numbers grew as the number of animals grew, and every morning we have to feed, water, clean out soiled bedding, and oversee rehomings and arrivals of abandoned creatures. Our vet bills almost crippled us, but then supporters started bequeathing us money, and we set up a website that enabled people to donate to us or sponsor an animal. We grew and grew, and now we have four hundred animals on the site with six or so coming in each day that need our help.

What people don't realize is that each sad case, each neglected, unwanted, unloved little soul that comes to us helps us in turn. I've seen volunteers with serious mental health problems blossom as they care for a damaged dog. I've seen people struggling with addictions come here and find they are useful and needed. Some people have been treated just as cruelly as the animals in their charge, and it forms a kind of healing symbiosis, a mutual compassion between human and beast, which transforms both their lives for the better.

We can't save every animal. Some arrive here with terrible undiagnosed diseases or with so much damage that they need to be given a merciful end to their lives. This is always the hardest part of what we do. We try to love each animal back to health, and we try very hard to give every animal a chance of life, but sometimes it is the kindest way. I've seen big, burly biker men break down in tears because the kitten they are caring for is so diseased it must be put down.

All human and animal life goes on here. I wonder each day at the unfathomable bond between people and animals, a connection that goes beyond words. When a broken, beaten, or starved animal comes to us and slowly gets better, it is a thing of beauty, a small miracle that we perform each and every day here at the sanctuary.

I have chosen to write about some of the dogs that have come to us because I want readers to come behind the scenes into this wonder. I want to show the challenges we face here, and also the joy and happiness that come from saving defenseless animals. It is an honor to have spent my life caring for them and being cared for in return.

Our motto here is encapsulated in this small prayer:

The FREEDOM we wish for all animals:

FREEDOM from hunger

FREEDOM from thirst

FREEDOM from neglect

FREEDOM from fear

It is my life's work to make this happen.

Barby

Chapter 1

TERRIFIED

The man towered over me with his fist raised, his shadow falling across my body as I lay in the small patch of earth I called home. I could hardly move at all as a chain was fastened too tightly around my neck, and wrapped around a post that stood solid and unmoving in a ditch a way back from his truck. It was a freezing cold winter's evening, and I was shivering as the night chill leached into my body.

Tentatively, I wagged my tail. Did he want to take me off my metal leash? Was I going to be fed? Would he pat me or stroke me, and tell me everything would be okay? They were always my hopes, but by now I should've learned that my hopes were always dashed, ground into dust before me.

I couldn't help it. I wagged my tail again, looking up at the man who terrified me, beseeching him, desperate for him to treat me kindly. After all, what had I done to deserve this confinement, a restriction so harsh for a greyhound like me who loves to run? I hadn't bitten anyone. I hadn't soiled my bed, though now it was hard not to as I couldn't move away from where I was forced to sit or lie. As a consequence I was smelly and covered in flies through the summer, cold and dirty through the drizzly autumn and harsh winter.

I panted with the strain of standing up. Recognizing his fury, I cowered beneath his dark gaze, feeling my long legs shaking with fear. I put my nose to the ground, my ears back. I was afraid for my life. He had beaten me mercilessly before, and since then I had known he was dangerous, that he was capable of almost anything.

This man was my owner, that much I knew. He was tall with a large, muscular body, thick stubble around his chin and large patterned tattoos adorning his skin. I whined a little, understanding that this wasn't a friendly visit, but then again, when had there been one since I'd been his dog? He had never bent down to say kind words to me. He had never fed me properly, throwing me scraps from his supper when he could be bothered. He had never let me run free, throwing sticks for me, or even walked me on the leash. But each time he came, I hoped and prayed that *this time* he would be kind, *this time* he would set me free, *this time* he would find some love for me in his hard heart. His face showed me otherwise.

I didn't know how long I'd been kept chained up in my outdoor prison, hungry and cold and desperate for some kindness and attention. It hadn't always been this way. I remember fleeting glimpses of excitement and freedom. Every time I smelled a hare or a fox's scent trails, it would ignite a spark, and in my mind's eye I would see the back of a hairy rabbit's body as it ran from me, feeling each muscle on my body strain and push to run toward it, my adrenaline pumping, my senses keen, sharper than an eagle's as I raced toward it.

I remember flashes of cheering crowds as the backdrop to my speed and agility. I remember the sight of the rabbit that produced such an intense focus, the surge of desire within me, creating the overwhelming urge to chase it, capture it, eat it. I was a hunter dog once, a fast, agile racer. I was unbeatable when it came to chasing smaller creatures, and I was given love and strokes, food, and kindness as a result. The people who cared for me back then were good to me, and I knew no different—until now. I am a loyal animal, I loved those who loved me with a sweetness and gentle happiness that is inherent in me. It makes my current owner's behavior all the more baffling—and frightening.

"Stand up, you mangy beast," he commanded, bringing me back to the reality of lying in a freezing ditch bound by a post and chains, a slave in all but name.

I hadn't eaten for days and was surviving on rainwater licked from the puddles next to me. I felt cold, weak and helpless. As I stood, straining against my incarceration, I moaned softly because I felt dizzy. That seemed to incense him.

"You bastard, you want bloody feeding, do you? Well, you haven't earned it yet, have you, eh? You don't deserve any of this nice supper." He signaled to one of the others nearby.

My nostrils went into overdrive. The smell of cooked chicken was suddenly overpowering as some of the food the men had been cooking over a campfire was tossed over to him and landed almost at my feet.

"Don't touch it!" he growled, walking the few paces over to me, kicking the food away with his boot. I hadn't dared touch it, even though I was faint with hunger. I knew the retaliation would outweigh sating myself with food.

Saliva formed around my mouth, strings of drool sliding downward, hanging from my tongue. The smell was all-encompassing, and it spoke to every cell and fiber of my being. I needed food. I was being starved and taunted, yet I knew I'd still do anything to make him love me enough to feed me.

It was almost unbearable. My empty tummy rumbled, my taste buds reeled from the smell of that cooked meat. I whined again.

It was the wrong thing to do. My owner seemed to double in size as he swayed slightly, standing over me, aware of his dominance and his power. I registered alarm, and lay myself flat against the cold ground again, hoping my show of deference would appease him. It only seemed to make him worse.

Suddenly, the man barked out a laugh entirely without mirth. He seemed to be finding the sight of me, drooling and desperate, funny. I couldn't understand why he would treat me this way. I wasn't racing anymore, so perhaps it was that? I just knew that since he'd become my owner, my life had not been worth living. Chained up twenty-four hours a day with sores on my neck from straining against the leash, and hungry to the point of fainting.

It was no way to live, and yet I couldn't escape. Suddenly there was a rustle from the undergrowth and I smelled the scent of a nearby fox. Even though my brain became alert to the prey, my body didn't follow this time. My heart didn't race with excitement and expectation. My concentration didn't follow, the tremble of sheer will and focus wasn't there. The urge to run that ran through my blood and bones had vanished. I was too sick and heartbroken to respond.

The man put his hands through his slick brown hair, and in doing so he seemed to lose his focus. He swayed again, and his eyes, which had been full of bitterness and rage, became unfocused for a moment. He recovered himself, stumbling on the mud beneath his feet, and a flicker of hope sprung up in my chest. Perhaps tonight I would escape a beating. Perhaps I could sleep without the pounding pain of the fresh wounds he inflicted upon me so regularly.

Each evening around this time, after the sun had set and the cold settled into my bones, the cries and laughter from the men who always hung around him would increase. Cans of drink would be passed around outside, no matter how icy it was, and they would talk and shout loudly, telling jokes, shoving each other playfully, and then, later, aggressively. I'd see the orange tips of their lit cigarettes dance in the gloom. As the evening wore on, they'd become louder and louder, and I'd feel more and more scared because I knew that before long I'd become the butt of some joke and the target of their frustrations.

My owner leaned down, planting his face in front of mine, his breath sour with alcohol and cigarettes, and said: "You won't be gettin' the back of my hand this time, bloody dog, but you watch out, do you hear me?"

I backed away as far as I could, nearer the wooden post that kept me pinned to this position, whimpering now. Then suddenly he was gone. He pulled a pouch of tobacco from his pocket, rolled a ramshackle cigarette, and fiddled about in his pockets for matches.

"Oi, you got a light there?" he shouted back to the crowd, his voice slurring as it did by this time most evenings.

"Nah, come over 'ere and get your light off the fire," one of the men barked back. "Leave that bloody dog alone. I don't know why you bother keeping it. It's no good to you now it can't race."

"Ahh, you're right, it's no bloody good to man or beast," my owner snorted back, the derision clear in his tone, before staggering away, leaving me lying there, blinking and silent, afraid to make a noise in case he returned.

My owner didn't just kick me with his heavy boots as he was passing. He didn't just throw a punch at my nose, making me yowl in pain. He didn't just hit me with whatever he was carrying in his hands—a newspaper rolled up, a piece of metal bar, a wooden post—leaving me scarred and bleeding. He did something that, for me, was far worse.

Laughing and jeering, he and his crowd of friends would stagger over with a bowl filled to the brim with food and leave it just out of reach. They'd sit down and casually smoke cigarettes as I strained and heaved my sore body to try to reach that plate. The tantalizing smell would send me half crazy. Every time I got too close they'd nudge it out of the way, chatting and sniggering, until I gave up and slunk back to a sitting or lying position, staring at them with blank eyes, unable to comprehend why they tormented me like this. I would be left to starve for days, and then, just as I would think they'd left me to die, someone would chuck me a bone or the remains of their meat dinner, and I'd wolf it down. Then it would start all over again.

The days were better. There were women and children milling around. Some of the children were cruel, and would copy their fathers by throwing rubbish or sticks at me, but a couple of the children were kind and would tell the others to "leave off him," though they never did.

Each morning and evening, I'd ask myself the same question: who here will love me? The answer was always the same: nobody.

Chapter 2

DUMPED

The days passed slowly. There had been little for me to do, little to see or enjoy, until now. Almost overnight, there was suddenly more movement around. People started coming and going, and in the midst of the renewed activity, I realized with a shock that my owner seemed to have forgotten me completely. He rarely came round to the back to see me, even to shout or rail at me anymore, and he seemed to have forgotten to feed me entirely.

I tried to sit up, but my body failed me. By now I was so starved that I could barely move. I felt woozy from hunger, but no food came. I smelled breakfast being cooked, the tobacco scent curling over the people as they came and went, and my mouth started to water even though I knew that no one would think of me, except to hurt me.

The dull pangs of hunger had sharpened into a pain that wouldn't subside. My body felt hollow, and I felt as light as air, as if I'd fly away if the chain wasn't weighing me down to the earth. My head would spin every time I moved, and even licking at the puddles that formed around my feet became a difficult chore. I knew it was the beginning of the end. I couldn't remember the last time someone had touched me or my body with love. I couldn't recall when someone was last kind to me, stroking my head, patting my body lightly, taking me for a walk, animal and human in gentle connection. All these things had gone forever, and I lay there waiting for my last breath to leave me.

Then one morning, just as I opened my eyes, the feeble winter sunshine seeming to blind me, my owner appeared. I barely registered him. I lay there, waiting to see what this encounter would bring me, my hopes and dreams of kindness completely vanquished now.

"You're not dead yet, then?" he barked, prodding me with his right boot. I whimpered. It was the only sound I could make now, and I didn't bother lifting my head. I didn't have the strength anyway.

He looked me over, scanning my body, his eyebrows raised. He seemed to pause, assessing me. I didn't care. My eyes started shutting. I didn't feel cold anymore. There was just a quiet humming inside my head, which I was still able to shake every now and then, to try to stop the noise but without much success.

"Oi, wake up, wake up, we're on the move."

Again, I barely acknowledged his presence.

My owner hesitated again. He was drawing hard on a hand-rolled cigarette, and he just stood there watching me. His face was in shadow. I couldn't see his expression, but by now I didn't care anyway.

I smelled the thick cloud of tobacco being blown toward me. He was standing inches from my head, his boots almost touching my ear. He could have dispatched me with one swift kick, or by stamping on my head. Part of me willed him to do it. I had no illusions that I would survive now. All my loyalty had been squashed and taken from me. I expected him to kill me now.

His lips curled in disdain. He seemed to hate my weakness, though he had brought me this low. He drew on the cigarette again, then, quick as lightning, he plunged it into my leg, stubbing it out on my body. A bolt of searing pain surged through me. I whimpered, because I didn't have the energy to cry out anymore. My owner laughed to himself, a deep growl of amusement at my reaction.

For a moment, the world went black and red as the agony ran its jagged path through my body. I tried to lick the wound but I couldn't raise my head and just watched as he turned tail and walked back to the others, whistling as he went.

Trucks and vans were being packed, and it was becoming clear that people were on the move. Some cars started to drive off, and I realized with a shock that I really would be left here. I didn't know which prospect was worse: to be taken with my owner, or to be left to die, alone and forgotten.

There was a loud shout from behind my owner's van. He headed in the direction of the voice, leaving me tied to the post, and I watched as he and two other men carried and lifted various things into his large van, laughing and joking as they did so. Doors slammed, people disappeared into their own vehicles, then, just as I was sure he would drive off without me, I heard the sound of his footsteps coming in my direction.

Horror struck. This would be it, the final moment. Would it hurt? Would I cry out? I started to tremble. The smell of his tobacco came closer and closer. Then I heard the strangest thing: the sound of metal sliding against wood. I peeped out of my closed eyes and saw my chain being unwound. Puzzled, I managed to lift up my head, unsure what was happening. Another man came close, and then I felt myself being scooped into his arms. I moaned. The cigarette burn still inflamed my leg, and every muscle and bone in my body seemed to be crying out in torment.

I didn't care what they were going to do with me. I knew from past experience that it wouldn't be good, couldn't be good.

Someone swore loudly. My ears were flat against my head in fear. I was jolted into my owner's arms and he slung me over his hip roughly like a sack of grain. I heard a car door open. My owner stepped inside the front passenger seat, my head knocking against the side of the car as we went. Again, I didn't care. All I wanted was a gentle word or a morsel of food or water—nothing else mattered.

The other man jumped into the front seat and started the ignition, the car reversing backward. I swayed on my owner's lap. He was holding me like I was trapped, rather than being comforted or embraced. The men began talking in low voices. My head started to play tricks on me—I swooned with exhaustion and starvation, going in and out of consciousness as the car made its way down muddy tracks and across main roads. I had no idea how long they drove or where we went. I was half-dead, fainting and shaking, muddled one minute then thankfully blank the next.

All of a sudden the car stopped. We'd arrived—but where? The wind howled, and the rain lashed down on me as soon as the car door was opened. I shivered. Where were we? What was happening? I whimpered, and that seemed to startle the men into action. Suddenly I was yanked out as my owner half walked, half ran to a metal gate with me in his arms. The sky was darkening, I could barely see anything but the gate and black trees surrounding it. None of this made sense, but before I could even think about what was next, I was hurled through the gate, thrown away like a rag doll, before crashing to the ground.

Everything happened so fast. I tried to get up. I stumbled. The scent of blood was in my nostrils. Was it mine? Then the odor of animals hit me. There were familiar scents of hare, rabbits, foxes, chickens, and others. A chorus of dogs started to bark from somewhere behind me.

The smell of the creatures awakened a dormant urge in me. I was suddenly the predator, no longer the prey. I felt a swift rise of desire and stood up, every sinew in my body wanting to chase the chickens, geese, and ducks I saw before me. But as soon as I tried to put one foot in front of the other, I started to wobble. Then everything went black.

Chapter 3

RESCUED

It was just past 6:30 a.m., and it was still as dark as night. Hundreds of gulls screeched and swooped over my head as I walked slowly down to the bottom of the field at the back of my bungalow. Since starting the sanctuary, I had always fed the birds that squawked, weaved, and glided over my land, believing that no creature, furry or feathered, would go hungry as long as I was around.

I started off with a handful of birds—pigeons and gulls mostly—that pecked the few slices of bread I shared with them after my breakfast. Clearly the birds were chatterboxes, because every day there seemed to be more and more joining in with the morning feast—crows, herring gulls, and jackdaws, to name a few—as well as smaller garden birds, all of them grateful for a morsel to eat from the crumbs left by the larger birds.

The birds hovered over me, caterwauling and crying to each other. The gulls were raucous, the crows guttural and earthy, while the garden birds chirped and sang. The braver

crows and gulls hopped onto the backs of the horses that stood
in the field next door. They carried on chewing and cropping
the grass and straw, seemingly oblivious to the pandemonium
surrounding them.

None of the birds ever touched me, yet they trusted me
completely. They never attacked me either, which was strange
as I was carrying a crate filled with sixteen loaves of torn-up
bread and was entirely alone in the chill of the bleak December
morning. The skies were dark as Hades, and the weather looked
set to turn nastier, so I was glad I could feed the scrawny creatures that gathered as I walked.

Early morning mist swathed the outlying hills and pas-
tures, making the birds appear ghostly in the gloom. My only
view was of the tips of the trees amid the fields and paddocks
that made up the Barby Keel Animal Sanctuary, all twelve
acres of our land. I knew the day would be busy in the buildup
to our annual Christmas Bazaar, and so I took the time to stay
with the theater of the feeding time, as if it had been staged
just for me. I felt something that was beyond words when I
saw the birds flying free. They'd take off in a great swarm of
wings, feathers, and beaks, flying high into the sky and off
over the green fields of the Sussex countryside. Every morning
I'd watch them leave. Rain or shine, I'd wait until every last
bird had continued on its way. It was a spectacle—and today
was no exception.

My spirits lifted as I went on with my daily duties, caring
for the four hundred residents we had currently, a task that
rooted me firmly to the soil. It was a feeling of complete com-
munion with nature in all its forms. However, before long my

head would be spinning with the number of duties that had
to be completed around the site before the day officially began.
I had to organize the feeding of our two hundred cats, which
meant more than one hundred cans of cat food needed to be
opened. There would be two hundred dishes to wash, two
hundred bowls of drinking water to be replenished, and this
all had to happen twice a day. On top of that we had six dogs
that needed to be walked, fed, and watered as well. Then there
was the telephone that rang twenty or thirty times a day, and
had to be answered, messages taken, transport arranged to
bring unwanted animals into the shelter, or to take them out
to be rehomed; sick animals had to be tended to and taken to
the vet, and all the medication had to be given out to those
creatures that were too ill to live anywhere but with us. And
on top of all that, there were people to match with animals.
I always had a list churning around my head: the names of
people and which animals they wanted to give a loving home
to, and the animals themselves that came in at the rate of six
or seven a day. It felt like a never-ending to-do list, especially
when I had to call up vendors and organize a raffle and the
publicity for our bazaar on top of everything else.

When I formalized the sanctuary charity, I vowed that we
would keep animals alive unless it was cruel to do so. I had
many beasts here with behavioral problems or illnesses that
meant they could never be rehomed, and I felt strongly that
they were entitled to a life here, living until they died naturally
in a place that showed them love and kindness, gave them a
soft clean bed, and kept their tummies full.

It was nice just to pause for a moment and take in the

beauty and chaos of the scene—a chance to reflect on why I'd
run the sanctuary for so long. It wasn't the easiest task, overseeing a team of volunteers, all the fund-raising efforts on behalf of the animals, and looking after the creatures themselves.
It required patience (which wasn't my strongest quality—ask
any of my motley crew), and trust, which again I have to work
hard at, as I often find myself believing that things are only
done properly when I do them myself, which generally means
I have worked fourteen-hour days, every day, since I came to
this place at the age of thirty-six.

Yet, my worries and cares, the burden of finding the money
to support us all, always fell away when I looked at those extraordinary, otherworldly creatures that flew into my life for
the sacrament of breakfast. Looking after animals was part of
my soul. I wouldn't have been me without this responsibility.
I'd dedicated my life to the care of them, to loving them, and
I recognized that perhaps I needed the beasts of sky and land
as much as they needed me.

"You'll catch your death out there. It's freezing," said Di,
wandering through the back door and inspecting me with a
frown.

Diane, a well-built lady of sixty, with long blonde wispy
hair covered almost permanently in a woolly hat, was one of
the longest-serving members of my team. She'd joined as a
volunteer more than thirty years ago and was now a trustee
of the charity and my most dependable worker and friend.

She was making her morning cuppa, using the urn I'd in-
stalled while I nursed my dad through his last illness.

"Want one?"

"Go on then, dearest." I usually waited until Dan arrived for his breakfast, but it was so damned cold out there it was hard to resist.

"Do we know what's happening today?" Di asked, handing me the steaming-hot tea.

"Too much is happening, that's what," I grumbled. Diane looked pointedly at my cup as I stirred in four teaspoons of sugar.

"Don't look . . ." I laughed as Di shook her head.

"All that sugar is bad for you, but you don't need me to tell you that," Di replied, her eyebrows raised.

Ignoring her advice, I took a sip, savoring the sweetness as it reached my taste buds, waking them up with a jolt.

"Some chickens have been dumped by a farmer who has sold up his farm. We need to rehome them, as I've got so many already here," I sighed.

Diane knew I was only moaning for the sake of it. All the staff knew my ways. I was fierce when it came to protecting animals, and I'd been known to refuse rehomings when I wasn't 100 percent sure about the intentions of the new owners. I'd got myself into trouble so many times with my fiery nature, but I knew where my heart lay, and it was always, always with the animals in my care.

"A flock of sheep is due in tomorrow, and I need to check with Dan that we have the proper Defra licenses . . ." At the sound of his name, the sanctuary farm manager, Dan, walked in, the strong wind banging the door shut after him.

"Mind you shut the door, Dan," I barked, winking at him.

"All right, Barby," he replied, a twinkle in his eye.

Dan was an extremely affable chap, absolutely committed to the animals here. He had volunteered with us for eight years before taking on the job, and he was as trustworthy and hardworking as they came. He was a tall man with curly dark hair and a very calm manner. Many a time he'd been the one to get me out of trouble. Once he'd had to stop me from marching out with a spade to bash a car belonging to someone who was living nearby at the time when I heard they'd complained about the noise our animals made.

"What do they bleedin' expect, living near an animal sanctuary?!" I'd shouted at the time, my face set, my temper rising with each footstep. Dan, who had been passing, luckily saw I was about to explode and so steered me back indoors.

"You can't go round threatening people or their cars with a spade," he'd said, calmly grabbing hold of my shoulders. With me a diminutive woman at five foot, Dan towered above me at more than six foot, but when my rage was ignited, I had the power and courage of a woman twice my height and half my age.

"I just wanted to make some more noise for them to complain about," I'd said as if it made perfect sense, to which Dan chuckled, making me even angrier.

"You won't solve anything like that. Come in, Barby, there's loads of digging you could do with that spade."

That was years ago, and the person I was angry with has long since departed, but my temper remains volatile where the welfare of animals is concerned. I am known for it, and this passion is why the sanctuary has been so successful: people know the animals are the heartbeat of this place, the very core of everything we do.

"What did you want me for, Barby?" asked Dan, putting two thick slices of whole-wheat bread in the toaster. People were wandering in now to make tea or breakfast and take shelter from the rain. Within minutes, it was lashing against the windows.

"Do you know anything about the sheep and their Defra licenses?" I asked.

Laid-back Dan shrugged his shoulders. "It'll all be fine. Don't worry yourself, we can handle all that."

"But I do worry," I replied, "and I've got a million other things to worry about as well today. I haven't got all the prizes in for the raffle so I need to ring round everyone who offered to donate them, and I've got to sort these chickens and get them matched up to someone, and . . ."

"Don't worry, Barby," Dan cut in, "it's all taken care of." I felt my face go red—the classic sign of me losing my temper.

"Barby, shouldn't you be looking after yourself?" Di stepped in. "You promised the consultant you would take it easy during this bout of cancer, so why don't you do just that? Dan here can organize everything. You have to learn to delegate, my dear."

I laughed at that.

"You're right," I sighed. My doctor had indeed given me strict instructions to stay away from stress and to spend time relaxing, as earlier in the year I'd been diagnosed with breast cancer for the second time. The new malignant tumor was sitting on the same spot as the first lump that I'd had removed five years previously. It had been a huge blow to hear my cancer had returned.

When my consultant had told me the news, which I already expected because I'd been through it before and knew having a biopsy meant cancer was suspected, he chided me for not following his instructions, that is, my refusal to have chemotherapy or take tamoxifen. At the time, I hadn't wanted any more "interference" from doctors, as I called it, but now that it had returned, I was left wondering if I had indeed done the right thing. The news didn't shock me like it had the first time, but, if anything, it was more frightening because I was older—and *felt* older. I'd never really returned to full health after the first cancer bout, despite having surgery to remove the lump. I hadn't regained my strength to do all the things I had done for the animals before, and my vulnerability and weakness had been a huge shock to me, resulting in me suffering from depression for a while after the operation.

So, my old enemy had returned—and, with it, yet another stay in hospital and another operation to remove it, though this time, thankfully, the surgery had been less invasive. It was too late to regret my past decisions; I had to carry on and just deal with what was in front of me.

My consultant Dr. Allen had insisted I go straight into surgery, but my stubborn side reared its head again, and I'd absolutely refused.

"You must go in soon, Barby. You have an aggressive tumor and we need to operate," he informed me rather sternly.

His tone didn't bother me. I knew my mind, and I knew that it would be hopeless to try to have surgery before the Summer Bazaar in August as I would be too stressed to recover, and my staff simply had enough on their plate without having me out of action as well.

I'd returned his gaze, and said: "No way, Doctor. My Summer Bazaar is the highlight of the year, and I must be there. We'll have to do the operation afterwards and that's my final word. I have a darts match on the Wednesday night before the bazaar, so I wouldn't have the surgery before then anyway, because it'll affect my throwing arm." Dr. Allen had given me one of his exasperated looks and sighed. It wasn't the first time I'd frustrated his attempts to cure me, and I could tell by the look on his face that he didn't know whether to laugh or tell me off.

"All right, Miss Keel, I know it's pointless arguing with you, and if you are going to be very stressed then it will affect your recovery. We will book you into Eastbourne Hospital for the operation the day after the bazaar, but you must promise to be there at eight on that Monday morning."

"Thank you, Doctor. I'll be there."

When the day of our bazaar arrived, my staff had built me a pen to sit in. I was literally contained like one of my farm animals with metal gates around me. This was to keep me from getting up and walking around, and also to make sure that people came to me rather than me to them. I knew it was a loving gesture, though an amusing one as I found myself in the position of one of my animals for once, but it served a purpose. However, despite the kindness and the good intentions of everyone around me, I couldn't help but feel useless, a feeling I had never liked. I was also anxious. There were always risks with surgery—I'd have been foolish to deny them. My dogs, Gabby, a honey-colored Lhasa Apso/Yorkshire terrier cross, and Harry, a large blond spaniel, were sitting by my side, and I'd kept a hand on each, stroking them and feeling their soft warmth against me. If anything had happened to me, it would be my dogs who would suffer the most, and I'd hated the thought of not knowing who would care for them.

The sanctuary had been taken care of before my first operation, though rather hastily. I'd come to an agreement with my trustees that I would sell the land and bungalow and everything I had built up to the charity for £1. That way there would be no wrangling over my will, and the animals and their futures would be secure. I have never regretted that decision, and at least it brought me peace of mind.

"Okay, I think we're ready. Barby, are you up to this?" Diane looked at me, squinting in the sunshine. It was almost midday, and we were ready to let in the people who were already queuing in the lane.

"I'm as ready as I'll ever be," I answered, "though I don't like being hemmed in like this!"

"It's for your own good. Now sit there and try not to worry."

"All right, Di, you win, I'll take it easy today, but I'll be watching you lot like a hawk, so you'd better make sure you do it all properly."

Di raised her eyebrows and Dan chuckled. They never took

me seriously, because they knew my heart was in the right place.

Di was right, but it was impossible to keep the trepidation from my mind the day before major surgery. I was grateful for the love of my dogs that afternoon as people filed in, and I cuddled Gabby up on my lap. However sad or worried I felt, I always drew comfort from my animals. That instinctive bond went beyond words and was infinitely comforting and reassuring. Gabby turned to me, her amber-flecked eyes looking up at me as if to say, "It'll be okay, Mum."

"I know, Gabby, I know. . . . I'm just a bit scared that's all."

When Gabby had arrived at the sanctuary, she was the most timid, frightened creature I think I'd ever seen. I went out to collect her from the car she'd been brought in and found her huddled and shaking on the floor of the back passenger side. I'd kept her in my bathroom, contained by a baby gate, to try to ease her into her new surroundings, but it took many months for her to build up the trust that any animal (or human for that matter) needs to thrive. She got there in the end, with much patience on my part and courage on hers. That day of the bazaar, it felt like our positions had reversed. I was the one trying not to shake in fear while Gabby looked at me with her steady, loving gaze, reassuring me in her own adorable way.

Despite my forebodings, I put on a brave face as our visitors were expecting a nice afternoon, and we had to give it to them—the charity funds relied upon it.

Friends and supporters flocked through the sanctuary gates all afternoon, and I soon realized the wisdom of putting me in the shade, sitting in my own little area as everyone seemed to want to speak to me, offering their best wishes and sympathy for the next day's surgery. Many people knew my cancer had returned as the local paper, the *Bexhill Observer*, had run a story about it. So many people came up to me, giving their support, telling me I'd be fine; it was wonderful to receive such blessings, but also very tiring. As the afternoon wore on, I remained seated more and more often, feeling like a queen on her throne watching her worker ants hurry around. I've always liked to be in the thick of the action, never one to stand at the sidelines, so I was almost relieved when the day ended.

My hospital bag had already been packed, and as soon as the bazaar was over, I was told in no uncertain terms to go and rest before my friends Elaine and Rob came to collect me to drive to the hospital first thing in the morning.

That was just under four months ago. I'd started a course of radiation therapy earlier in the month, and was surprised at how weak and tired it had left me, though considering I had to get to Brighton Hospital every weekday for the treatment, perhaps that wasn't surprising. Some mornings, like today, it was a struggle to get up and out of bed at all, but I knew it was worth it. Feeding the birds also fed my soul, it was as simple as that.

The day passed in a blur of activity, set against the pelting rain and howling wind. By late afternoon, the sky was black, and nightfall was on its way. The wind and rain had picked up once more, and I shivered inside, telephoning supporters and generally getting on top of all the admin for the Christmas Bazaar before the inevitable crash as the effects of the radiation

therapy hit me. At that point, it was all I could do to crawl
to bed with Gabby and Harry. Being so sick brought back
painful memories of both my father and my brother's illnesses
and subsequent deaths; lying in bed gave me too much time
to spend with my thoughts as I lay there each evening, exhausted and spent after doing even the most minor of sanctuary jobs.

My brother Peter had been the golden child at home. I had
tried very hard to resent my older brother for it, but I couldn't.
He was the apple of my eye too, a blond-haired, blue-eyed
smiling sweet boy whom I revered, though he played a few
tricks on me in his time. When we were evacuated during the
war, we were playing in a field when Peter suggested I try
one of the "chocolate pies" lying flat in the fields. Needless
to say, I did and got a nasty shock. While evacuated, my
mother made me sleep on two chairs pulled together while
Peter had the only bed. I resented my mother for the way she
treated me, though I was always clean, well dressed, and well
fed, but I couldn't hate my brother for the attention he received. In fact, I agreed with Mum that he was the handsome
favorite. As a child, I had tangled brown hair that I refused
to brush and a permanent scowl on my face, and I used to
scuff my shoes and play in the dirt just to annoy my mother.
I was the ugly duckling to Peter's swan. Peter developed
leukemia in his fifties and died far too young.

I thought of him as the sky darkened. He had been in pain.
He had spent weeks in the hospital. He had known what it
was to face his own death, and I couldn't help but pity him.
I still missed him deeply, even though it had been many years

since his death; the same for my father, whom I had nursed at home in the bungalow through his last months. My musings were broken by the sound of an urgent voice carried by the wind outside.

"Barby, come quickly, we need to cover the haystacks," Di panted, running inside my bungalow. "The wind has blown the tarpaulin off, and we need as many hands as possible! I know you need to rest, but there's only a few of us here. Come quickly."

Without a word, I ran out as fast as I could, trying to ignore the pain from the surgery scars. They still hurt, and overnight the pain had worsened and become a searing, throbbing agony, so I'd slept badly. When I'd checked myself in the morning, I could see the beginnings of a harsh red welt along the length of the scarring. Shocked, I hadn't yet confided in anyone. I knew I should probably have rung the hospital to check if this reaction was normal after radiation therapy, but there was always so much to do, and my health concerns tended to be less of a priority as animals came in. I was never one to court sympathy. I wanted always to be there when I was needed; I couldn't let the others—or the animals—down. If we lost the hay, our winter feed stocks would be threatened, and we'd have to spend money we could ill afford on new hay. I had to help.

The rain hit my face as I ran as fast as I could while clutching my left side under my winter coat. I almost slid on the wet grass.

"This way!" shouted Diane.

Dan was there too. Di had clearly called Fran and Christine on their walkie-talkies, and the pair of them, who looked after the kennels together, hurried toward us to help.

Together we began the task of grappling with the flapping plastic covering that was slapping against our faces as we tried to grab it. Eventually Fran caught it, and we all took a corner, holding it down. The wind was now gale force, and it was a struggle to keep hold of the material.

Just as we seemed to have the situation under control, we heard the sound of the large bell at the entrance, only just audible above the scream of the wind. It clanged and clanged.

"What's going on?" I shouted above the storm.

Dan was hanging onto the rope and trying to tie the material back down, so I looked to Diane. She shrugged.

"We'd better find out," I cried, rain splattering my face.

Di was first to get to the yard that made up the entrance to the sanctuary. I ran after her, my heart pounding and my legs feeling like jelly now. I felt faint, suddenly realizing the toll the cancer and the operation had taken on my body.

Ahead of me, I saw Di stop abruptly. She was shouting something to someone, but I couldn't hear her above the downpour.

Then in front of me I saw a dark shape, like a skeleton with skin stretched over it. It was floundering, staggering around the yard.

"It's a greyhound. He's been dumped through the gate." Di's face was contorted with shock and horror. "Tessa, one of the volunteers, saw the men drive in. They dumped the poor creature and then they jumped in their car and drove away." Di, who was normally a placid soul, was shouting furiously.

"Is it . . . is it . . . a dog?" I asked in disbelief, watching helplessly as the shape zigzagged alarmingly. I was overcome with an emotion I could barely name; a mixture of sadness, disbelief, and revulsion. The poor thing had been starved, that much was clear. It looked like death warmed over. My instinct told me that this creature would not survive the night.

As though to confirm my fear, the hound keeled over like a drowning vessel at sea, collapsing to the ground. I ran straight over, but Di got there first. She peered down at him, running her hands along the length of his emaciated body.

My gaze swept over the stricken animal. It was more skeleton than animal. I knelt down in the wet and started to feel over his body, which was slick with rain and grime. Di moved away and let me feel his black fur. I could touch every rib, every bone. The fur that covered his haunches was patchy and missing in so many places. I felt sickened to the pit of my stomach.

Just then, as everyone else arrived, the dog started to come round again. I murmured soft words to him, trying to reassure him that he was safe, that everything would be okay, but my heart had sunk to my boots. Clearly he wasn't okay at all. I felt I was looking death squarely in the face as I gazed at this once-graceful animal.

I stroked his ears, trying to reassure him. Perhaps the worst part was that once he'd registered my touch, he cringed back from me, as if he was expecting a beating. I'd seen it before with other animals, that split-second bolt of fear, and every time it hit me hard. It was clear proof of the cruelties that must have been inflicted on him, and it was all I could do to keep my emotions under control.

"You're safe, my darling, you're safe here with us. We'll all look after you," I crooned as if to a newborn baby, and under my breath I added, "if you don't die before morning."

Chapter 4

SHOCKING DISCOVERY

"Get him inside, quick!" I shouted, looking up at Di, Fran and Christine.

Together, we lifted the dog up to standing position and half walked, half carried him to the kennels, holding him with absolute tenderness, gingerly moving in sync with this stricken creature. His bones were so prominent we were all terrified of injuring him further. His skin looked so stretched and sore, we were afraid to touch him, but touch him we must if we were going to help him in any way.

"We have to get him out of this rain and wind. He's on the brink of death," I shouted above the maelstrom.

Christine nodded, then peered at me, saying: "You don't look so hot yourself, Barby. Why don't you go inside and have a lie down?"

"Not until we can get him somewhere safe and warm," I called back, though Christine was right, I wasn't feeling well at all. The pain in my side had built from a throbbing to a red-hot pounding. It was so strong that I thought for a moment I was going to faint. I felt cold sweat on my brow, and my body was now aching and longing for rest.

Stay with it, Barby, don't give up now, you've got to help this poor boy . . . I said to myself, willing myself to have the strength to help this desperate animal. I had to focus on his needs, on his pain, and not my own, although that was very, very difficult.

As we staggered across the yard to the kennels, I had to concentrate on breathing or I really might have passed out.

Keep going, keep going, old girl . . . I said to myself as a kind of mantra.

I didn't know if the dog or I was more grateful to see the inside of the shelter. By now he was moaning softly and appeared to be coming in and out of consciousness. During those rare moments of lucidity, he'd turn his head and peer up into my eyes, boring into them with a sadness that took my breath away. His eyes were black and dull—the life seemed to have almost leached from them completely. What terrible deeds had been done to this poor animal? What secrets did his eyes hold? It broke my heart to know that he had suffered, and was still suffering.

"Shhhh, there, boy. It's all going to be okay now. We've got you," I said, stroking his patchy, mangy fur as gently and soothingly as I could. "Look how many people are here to help you. You'll be better in no time at all, just hang in there, boy . . ."

I couldn't stop my voice from cracking with emotion. I

cleared my throat. It wouldn't do to break down now. I would
have to wait until I was alone. Seeing how weak he was, how
thin and starved he'd become, meant the chance of him surviving the night was slim.

I could see that he would've been a handsome hound, despite his gaunt appearance. His fur was a deep charcoal-gray
color, shot through with black, but because it was getting
dark, it was difficult to pinpoint his exact coloring. His gentle
eyes looked at me with something like intelligence, but the
light in them kept flickering out, and I knew we didn't have
much time to save him.

We got him through the doorway and into the emergency
kennels. They had only recently been built after the sanctuary
was left a legacy for exactly this kind of situation. In these kennels we had basic medical supplies, warm blankets, and food
in case we got called overnight to collect an abandoned dog.

I'd seen many dogs brought in here after suffering, at best,
questionable handling, and at worst, downright neglect and
abuse. But this was by far the most extreme case I'd ever come
across.

"You okay, Barby?" said Di quietly. She was standing next
to me, her face showing concern in the dim light of the kennel.
She knew me better than I knew myself at times, and she'd
obviously noticed how pale I must've become even in those
few short paces. I nodded my response, suddenly feeling dizzy,
and biting my lip, drawing blood, a metallic taste filling my
mouth.

To deflect my friend's attention away from me, I fell back
on my position as founder of the sanctuary, taking control of

the situation and raising my voice, calling out instructions to the others.

"Get him a towel and some water, quickly. . . . Yes, that's it, rub him down very gently, we have to make sure we get him through the night."

It was a relief to see how quickly my mind went onto autopilot. While in charge, I stopped worrying about myself, and just got on with the job in hand: saving this shockingly brutalized dog. We were on a life-or-death mission that night.

"Fran, will you see if he'll take a small spoon of dog food? Try the puppy one, as it's kinder to sore tummies. There isn't a shred of meat on this poor chap's bones. I don't know how he's still alive, I really don't."

Christine nodded her head. Her face reflected my feelings. She looked subdued and close to tears herself. I don't think any of us could understand the depth of cruelty that this greyhound must have endured. It was almost beyond belief, and at a shelter like ours that takes in unwanted, abused, and unloved animals on a daily basis, that was really saying something.

We were all professionals, though. We had to work together to help him, and already my volunteers and staff were buzzing around in harmony looking after this dog. For a moment, I surveyed the scene: Fran dishing out dog food, Diane holding the dog, gently stroking him as Christine wiped him softly with a clean, dry towel to dry him off.

He was now lying on the dog bed we kept in there, his face flat on the fabric, staring at the wall, panting like it was an effort. The darkness and the tempest raging outside mirrored the emotional drama unfolding at the heart of the sanctuary tonight.

Christine gently dabbed the dog: "It was the softest towel I could find. We don't want to make his skin worse. . . . Now come on then, we don't even know your name, Mr. Greyhound."

Christine was a dog lover just like me. She'd volunteered with us for years, starting by walking a dog or two, and was now running the kennels alongside Fran, who also worked at the cattery. She was a wonderful woman, always calm in a crisis and kind to everyone, animals and people alike. She had blonde hair tied back in two pigtails that framed her lovely face, though the rain had left her looking just like the rest of us, like a truly motley crew of drowned rats.

"Let's call him Bailey, after my favorite tipple," I said stoutly. I didn't know where the name had come from, it just popped into my head.

"Okay, Bailey, I think that's a perfectly good name for now, don't you?" crooned Christine. He raised his head off the bed and blinked at her before settling back down again.

"I think he's approved it!" laughed Christine softly. "I just hope you're still with us tomorrow, Bailey."

"Did anyone get a proper look at the men who did this?" My anger had reared up like a striking snake, and I was suddenly desperate to find the perpetrators. Di shook her head.

"I'll kill them, I will!" I vowed, realizing I was trembling, perhaps with delayed shock, perhaps with the pain that I was battling, but mostly with the rage that I'd suppressed up to this moment. It had been more important to get Bailey to safety than it was to vent, but now I was free to feel the true depth of my distress.

"I promise you, I'll kill the lot of them if I ever set eyes on them," I snarled, but as usual it was Dan, who had arrived in the middle of the melee after spending the last hour or so securing the hay cover back down, who calmed me down.

He placed a hand on my shoulder. "Save your energy for this boy here," he said wisely.

Just then I spotted the burns on Bailey's legs. "Those are cigarette burns, aren't they? They're bloody cigarette burns on the dog's legs. How can anyone be so vicious? How?" Hot, angry tears sprang to my eyes, obscuring my vision, though I still saw Dan and Christine exchange a look between them.

"I can see you both. I know I need to calm down, but I just can't. When people hurt animals then that's me gone. . . . I wouldn't care if they put me in jail for it." I was visibly shaking now.

Di stepped in, her placid tones bringing me back to my senses a little.

"They drove off in a car," she said. "But I was so worried about the dog and the chickens I didn't get a chance to look at it. I'm sorry, Barby." Di looked anguished.

"I know it wasn't your fault, dearest." I sighed deeply.

"It was a good thing I never got to see them. They'd have probably been bashed over the head with a spade if I had. Dan wouldn't have been able to stop me."

Dan chuckled at that: "You're right about that, Barby. You are a force of nature—not even this storm is a match for you!"

I managed a weak smile at that.

"He was left to die," I said flatly, the drama of the past ten minutes or so starting to take its toll.

Fran nodded. "Though they had just enough heart to dump him here, don't forget. They could have left him wherever they had stayed, or they could have drowned him. At least bringing him here was the right thing."

Fran often saw the bigger picture when it came to the sanctuary, much like Dan. Fran had been with us for a few years now and was a staunch animal rights campaigner. He was a strong, stocky man who was often called upon to bridle the wild horses that we saved. He was fearless in the face of all animals, and worked both in the kennels and the cattery with Christine.

I couldn't argue with what he was saying. The previous owners could just have killed him themselves, or dumped him somewhere to die where he wouldn't have been found. They had done this dog one great kindness at least.

I took charge again, asserting myself back over the situation. I had to remember that our only focus should be looking after Bailey—everything else was secondary.

"He needs water fed to him from a teaspoon. It's too late to call the vet out," I said, looking at my watch, "so we'll have to keep him alive till morning and then see what Stephen says."

Stephen White was the local vet from the Claremont practice in nearby Sidley who we used for all our domestic animals, and I knew his reaction would mirror mine: utter disbelief and shock. He was a man who clearly adored animals of all shapes and sizes, and he often came to us to save us the effort of trekking up the lane with a sick creature, so we all held him in high esteem.

"Go inside, Barby, you still need to recuperate. You look pale," Di said, and this time I knew there was no point in resisting. I was indeed shattered. I felt wobbly on my feet, and the pain was throbbing insistently.

I nodded, all fight having left me, and reluctantly turned to go, casting a final look over to Bailey, who lay motionless in his bed, every bone of his emaciated frame highlighted by the low light. I shuddered. "Do what you can for him, please," I said to no one in particular, shutting the door behind me.

Walking slowly back to my bungalow, which sat at the heart of the site, yards away from the entrance and the kennels, I knew that no matter what we did for Bailey that night, only luck and a strong will on his part would save him now. I also knew I wouldn't sleep a wink after the horrors I'd witnessed.

As soon as I was safe in the sanctuary of my bedroom, I felt tears prick my eyes. I was sore, exhausted, and overwhelmed by the cruelties that Bailey must have suffered. I wandered into my small bathroom that connected to the bedroom and looked at myself in the mirror. I was a woman of seventy-three with white-gray hair pulled back off my face. I'd put on weight since my last surgery and still looked a healthy size. Wrinkles framed my eyes, which were red from tiredness, and soon the tears started to flow freely.

Carefully, I took off my work clothes, leaving them in a heap on the floor. Harry and Gabby greeted me as I entered, then leaped back onto the bed, both already yawning and preparing to settle down for the night. I pulled on a T-shirt, inspecting my sore body for the last time. The welt looked, if anything, a little better, though it still throbbed. Lying down, I felt the dogs' warmth beside me, their breathing and snuffling indicating they were drifting into sleep. For me, however, it was going to be a long, long night.

Chapter 5

VET'S ASSESSMENT

In a "normal" situation when an animal comes into the sanctuary, there are specific procedures and processes that must be undertaken to hand over the rights and responsibilities of the pet. Every person who comes in has to fill out one of our forms to assign their rights over the animal to us at the Barby Keel Animal Sanctuary. Dog owners fill out different forms from cat owners, and farm animals such as cattle, pigs, deer, goats, and sheep are subject to a Defra Movement General License, which means we have to follow strict government guidelines for the transportation and change in ownership of the animals.

Usually, when someone comes to the sanctuary asking us to take their pet, they have to complete an exhaustive set of questions detailing every aspect of the animal they are being forced through circumstance to give up. The form asks health questions such as whether the animal has been neutered or spayed and whether it has received any veterinary treatment, and there are also extensive questions about their pet's behavior and if they have any problems arising from that. For example, we have to ask if a dog has been the subject of any police or court involvement. We also like to understand whether the animal plays with toys and responds to commands, what kind of food it likes, where the dog was obtained—for instance, whether it was a stray or adopted from another animal shelter, or whether it was bought as a puppy—and the kind of family or home environment it was coming from. All of the answers given, assuming they are given truthfully, help to build up a picture of a dog's overall well-being, what it was used to, and whether we would need any specialist training or help with obedience.

We have seen some sorry stories here. People were being told by rogue landlords that they couldn't keep their pets in the rental properties any longer. Many a time, we'd seen the devastation caused by, in my view, these heartless conditions for tenants who had little power to complain. People were being told, "It's you or the cat."

Giving up an animal is often an extremely painful decision, especially if the pet is still loved and wanted. For many people, their pet is more than just an animal: it's a companion, a trusted friend, a creature that gives meaning to their lives. Being told to leave their home because of the pet was therefore an absolute tragedy, but one we were seeing more and more often.

Sometimes an animal's expenses can become overwhelming, with veterinary bills and increases in the cost of living, meaning that poverty is another reason for the rising tide of animals being abandoned.

Circumstances can change. People struggle with pets with behavioral problems, particularly when they might need unforeseen expensive medical treatment or training as a result.

But of course none of these things applied to the emaciated and neglected greyhound who would be lucky to survive the night. As the darkness turned to daylight, and I lay there staring at the ceiling, sleep eluding me, I wondered why those men had brought Bailey to me in the end. They could have left him for dead and gotten away with it. There was no benefit to them in leaving him here. In fact, they had risked being identified on our CCTV cameras, and yet in the end it was possible they may have saved his life.

On one hand, I was traumatized by how cruelly people can treat a beautiful dog like Bailey, but on the other hand, I was grateful to them for eventually doing the right thing. I felt such a mix of emotions. It was confusing to think I could be grateful to someone who had treated an animal so appallingly.

All night long, I couldn't get Bailey out of my head: the sight of him stumbling, his bones covered only in patches of skin that looked sore and painful, his tongue thick as it lolled out of his mouth. He was by far in the worst condition of any living creature I'd seen in all the years I'd run the sanctuary.

I lay there with Harry and Gabby beside me. Their presence usually comforting enough to help me drop off, but this night it didn't come close to soothing me. A couple of times in the night, Gabby would twitch her ears and look up at me, her brown liquid eyes full of love. She always knew when I was unsettled or upset, we were so in tune, but I had no words to share with her. I'd stroke her golden fur and shush her back to sleep. Harry was twice the size of Gabby and would snore and snuffle, twitching as his doggie dreams unfolded under his mop of light hair.

The light from daybreak was filtering through my curtains, and I knew it was high time to find out whether Bailey had survived the night. The storm had abated, though it was still cold and overcast. I shivered as I stepped out from the covers. Gabby shook herself all over and yawned while Harry immediately jumped down and headed to the back door, scratching at it until I let him out.

"You've got a perfectly fine dog exit by the front door, why don't you use that?" I muttered, turning the lock and opening the door a crack to let him out for his morning wee, Gabby close behind him. I watched them trot down toward the back field and smiled. When Gabby came to me after her owners became too ill to look after her, I learned she had never been outside. In her, then, eight years of life, she'd never done her business outside, she'd never learned to play, and, strangest of all, she hadn't yet learned to bark. It took me many months to coax her into doing all three, using every trick I knew. She got there in the end, and the resulting bond between us was unbreakable.

Harry had been a really naughty boy when he arrived. He would try to bite people, as well as other dogs, and so we really had to train him from scratch as well, though it wasn't until the arrival of my other dog, Ben, a laid-back, easygoing black Labrador, that he calmed down and became a lovely companion at last. Ben came to me after a long-serving volunteer had died and was with me for five years before he too passed away.

Ben had been a wonderful influence on Harry, who doted on him from the first time they set eyes on each other. Harry seemed almost to copy Ben, and, in doing so, he became more like him. When Harry was introduced to Gabby, it was also love at first sight. He'd been her protector, and had done a lot of her "training" himself. He would make sure Gabby was following close behind him once I'd coaxed her outside, and he stayed with her while she did her business. It really had been a remarkable journey with these two dogs—and now there was another one that desperately needed my help. I just hoped he was still alive for me to give it.

The kennels were still dark. Christine was leaning against the wall swaddled in a blanket, her eyes red-rimmed with tiredness, with Bailey's head on her lap. I tried to keep calm.

"Morning, Christine dearest. Well, you look like how I feel." I smiled grimly, trying to keep the fear out of my voice.

"Morning, Barby. Goodness, you don't look any better. Didn't you sleep either?" Christine asked.

I shook my head in response. I was more worried about the dog on her lap than my sleep deprivation. All my mental energy and focus needed to be on this poor creature.

"Sorry, dear, but I need to put the light on in here so I can check this boy over," I said.

I'd left Gabby and Harry indoors. It was far too cold for them out here, and I didn't want to alarm Bailey and cause him any more distress.

I flicked on the light.

"Hello, darling boy, oh you're still with us. What a clever dog you are . . . and well done, Christine," I said, meaning every word. Staying here overnight wasn't an easy task. It was built for a dog's comfort, not a human's, but despite this, my trusted friend and worker had stayed with Bailey all night. I couldn't have been more grateful to her.

Again, I couldn't help but be shocked. In the electric light I could see clearly the scars from cigarette burns running down his legs, the fur missing from malnutrition, and various cuts and bruises from what appeared to have been regular beatings. He was a skeleton held together by the skin stretched over his prominent bones. He had no fat on him at all. It was truly a wonder he was still alive.

"How did the night go?" I asked, not taking my eyes off Bailey. I knelt down next to them while my heart flooded with relief, seeing his thin body rising and falling with each breath. My knees were rather stiff these days, but I refused to molly-coddle myself. I felt as fit as a young woman in my heart, it was just my body refusing to cooperate.

"I've managed to give him tiny sips of water all through the night, and he's managed a couple of teaspoons of food. When the vet gets here, he'll most likely put him on the high-protein dog food—that way we can give him tiny amounts but it will all help to build him up," Christine said, smiling sadly down at the dog who lifted his head and gently licked her hand as she tickled his ears.

"You've done a marvelous job, dear. You must be shattered. Why don't I take over until Stephen gets here?" I said. I'd left an urgent message, asking him to get down here as we had a dog that was too ill to transport to the practice. I knew he'd come straight here even though it was a Saturday morning.

Christine shook her head. "You've got enough of your own things to worry about, what with your radiation therapy. No, I'll stay here until Fran gets in, and he'll take over until the vet arrives."

"Would everyone please stop going on about the cancer?" I exclaimed, rather more defensively than I'd intended. "I'm perfectly fine. They got the tumor out, and now I just have to get through this blasted treatment, then I'll be right as rain."

Christine just shook her head again, smiling. "Barby, I've never met a more obstinate woman. You're going to have to slow down, or you'll be no good to this poor chap if you're ill again."

At that, we both looked down at him. Bailey shifted, staring back at me beseechingly. I could see that when, *if*, he recovered, he would be a beauty, with black coloring and a long elegant face and neck speckled with white fur. He really was a dear creature. That made my mind up.

"I don't care what you say, Christine, I'm staying here with you and Bailey. I want to hear everything Stephen says. Now move over a little, I'll get him settled with me so you can make us both a cuppa."

"You're the boss," Christine laughed, getting up and yawning as she moved toward the kitchen area.

"I bleedin' well am, and don't you forget it," I grinned.

"Now then, Bailey," I said softly, "you've had a rough old life. Well, so have I in many ways, we've got a lot in common. Did you know my mother used to call me a grump and a rat-bag? Do you know why she did? Because I was, that's why!

"Mum used to adore my older brother, Peter. He was the perfect boy, the golden child, and do you know what? He really was. I loved him very much as well, but I didn't compare well to him, and so I got a lot of rough treatment from my mother. She was always cross with me for something, and I don't remember her ever giving me a cuddle. How sad is that, eh, Bailey? Don't suppose you've had many of those either, eh, boy?"

I murmured away to the animal as Christine busied herself, tidying up, getting out the cups, and nibbling at the stash of cookies kept for times like this when a trip out to the shops or bungalow for breakfast was just an impossible task. I stroked Bailey's thin fur, my fingers tracing his bony head and neck. Bailey turned his head to me. He had soulful eyes, dark as the night, and a gentle nature, that much was obvious.

Suddenly, to my surprise, the frail dog started to shift in my lap. With shaking legs, he managed to stand up. I stood up beside him. "I think he needs a wee," I called to Christine, who by this time was out the back.

"That's good news, means everything's in good working order. Okay, I'll come and help you take him out," she replied, appearing through the doorway.

Together we walked the unsteady dog out to the yard, where he was able to relieve himself. He already seemed a little stronger and could stand unaided for a few moments.

Once he'd finished, we led him back in, just as Fran arrived. I was just reaching out for the hot mug of tea Christine was holding out to me when suddenly the bell at the gate jangled. My heart shuddered from a momentary flashback to the events of the day before, but I quickly gathered myself.

"I'll go," I said stoutly, and Fran followed close behind me.

"How's he been?" he asked as we walked the few yards to the entrance.

"He's alive, and that's what counts, but I'm very glad the vet's here," I replied as I spotted Stephen on the other side of the metal barred gate.

"Sorry, Stephen, we hadn't unlocked yet," I called out as I turned the key.

"Now what's this about a starved dog, then, Barby? Is he very unwell?" Stephen asked as we turned to walk back to the kennels. There was no time for small talk.

Stephen was a very busy man. It was a testament to his professionalism that he'd come out early, before he was scheduled to see the other cases on his books. He was a wonderful vet, and we all trusted his advice implicitly.

"Yes, he was dumped here last night. I can't explain to you what state he's in—you'll have to see for yourself," I said, shaking my head.

Stephen was a man in his early forties with a serious expression and utter devotion to his work. He was usually so calm and steady, but, once inside the kennel, the shock of seeing the dog's condition was visible on his face.

I was pleased to see that Bailey had remained standing, though he was being supported by Christine as he'd lost so much muscle mass. Christine was holding his leash, but there was no need—he wasn't going anywhere anytime soon.

"Gosh, I see why you've been so worried, Barby. Well, of course, he's severely malnourished, you can see the fine coating of dandruff on his coat," he sighed, checking Bailey's ribs all over and listening to his heart with the stethoscope.

"He's riddled with tapeworm too, and we need to look at the sores on his legs. He's a real mess."

"Should we start feeding him some of the high-protein dog food?" asked Fran, who was listening from the doorway.

"Yes, give him a teaspoon at a time, but not too much, as his stomach needs time to adjust to regular feeds."

We all nodded. Bailey would need round-the-clock care, that much was obvious.

"I'll write up his prescriptions now. You know where I am if you need me," Stephen concluded.

"Thank you so much for coming straight out, Stephen. It was kind of you. I'll show you out," I said, grateful for the care Bailey would receive. It was clear we had a lot of work to do, but I felt a surge of optimism and felt sure that, together, we would help this painfully injured creature.

"It'll be a long, slow recovery," Stephen warned, his face grim. I nodded, but was thankful that Bailey was in exactly the right place now. I muttered a prayer under my breath: *Thank you, God, for making those people dump him here. Thank you for our wonderful vet, and for all the staff here. Please, God, let Bailey survive . . .*

Christine was leaving the kennels as I arrived back from seeing the vet off.

"Barby, I'm going home to get some sleep and a shower. I'll be back later today, and I'm very happy to sit with him overnight, but you can't stay with him all day long. You need to take care of yourself too, Barby." Christine gave me a stern look, but she'd been with me for years and knew how stubborn I could be.

"I can't promise you anything, dear, I just want to see Bailey get better. You know me, I never listen," I chuckled, waving her off.

Fran was now with Bailey, who was lying down again.

"Here, you let me have him while you go and get some of that dog food the vet recommended," I instructed. Fran doffed his cap in mock submission and walked off, whistling.

"There, we've got a few moments of quiet, just you and me, Bailey," I whispered, stroking his head gently. His ears flickered up but he looked exhausted, and he made no other sign he'd heard me. We sat together on his bed on the floor of the kennels. I knew I couldn't stay with him all day despite what I'd said to Christine. I needed to call the hospital about my own pains, and there were other responsibilities to attend to across the site, but for a few precious moments we sat there, both of us tired almost to death. I stroked his gaunt head and neck, and suddenly Bailey shifted, and, moving his head slowly round, he licked my hand. Such a simple gesture, yet it meant the world to me. In that moment, I saw his bravery, his ability to trust me even though he had received so little kindness in his life.

That moment became one of harmony between us. He shut his eyes and moved his head back, settling down to sleep on my lap.

For me, the small gesture of affection created a glimmer of hope, a beacon of light that carried me through the coming weeks.

Chapter 6

SLOW PROGRESS

Standing in the kennels, I watched Bailey struggle to get up by himself. It was two days after he'd been unceremoniously dumped, and, despite taking in the water and tiny portions of food offered, he was still extremely weak.

I frowned. The injustice of it beat at my brain. I was furious that the perpetrators of these crimes were walking around scot-free. Bailey looked over at me, his face a picture of sadness, his limbs shaking beneath the barely there weight of his frail body.

Something inside me snapped. I needed to know more—even just to *have* the knowledge rather than *use* it. I didn't know if justice would be served by finding the previous owners—some things were, perhaps, best left alone. After all, they'd done such brutal things to Bailey, how would I, a seventy-three-year-old woman, stand up to them? But these thoughts wouldn't stop—and I knew myself well enough to know that I would always wonder about it if I didn't take some sort of action.

Christine had said she would stay with Bailey overnight, so I knew he was in safe hands. That meant that I could go back to my bungalow and start a plan of action. I knelt next to the thin hound, and, taking his face in my hands, I vowed that I would find out everything I could about his past, even just to understand rather than to do anything about it.

Bailey's beautiful eyes stared back at me. His expression was unfathomable. He trembled as I spoke to him and I realized he was still in shock, perhaps still thinking that we would turn on him. The thought made me feel physically sick.

"All right, boy, I won't hurt you," I soothed gently. "I'm going to go and see what I can do about tracing your background. Christine is here now to look after you. You've got nothing to worry about. There's no danger here, you're safe with us, Bailey, I promise you."

I didn't know if my words made any sense to this poor creature. His ears flicked back, expectantly. If he was used to daily violence and cruelty, then it would take him a long time to learn to trust us—and believe he was safe.

Stroking his head gently one last time, I stood, my mind made up. I strode decisively back toward the house and settled down at the table.

"What are you doing, Barby? And how's Bailey?" Di asked, startling me as she ambled into the living room. Her bobbly hat was slightly askew, giving her a rather rumpled appearance. Her hair was in strands around her face, and her cheeks looked pink with exertion.

"The question is, what have *you* been up to?" I chuckled.

Di grinned. "I've been helping Harry to move some of the

cement mix for the pathway. I couldn't let him struggle on his own, could I? You know I like being useful. Anyway, I asked the question first, what are you doing?"

"I've decided to make a poster to put up around Bexhill and the surrounding area. I want to find out who Bailey's owners were," I explained. "One of the volunteers took a photograph of him when he arrived, and I'm using that to create a very hard-hitting poster. If this doesn't unearth those *people*," and at that I spat out the word, "then nothing will."

"You be careful, Barby. You know what you're like with your temper. You watch you don't go stirring things up. Perhaps it's best to let things be, and just focus on helping Bailey," Di said.

"I know what you're saying, Diane dearest, but I can't help myself. I want to know everything I can about that greyhound and the life he's had. The poster may prompt people's memories, or bring a neighbor or landowner to the surface who may have more information," I told her firmly, though Di had a good point. Sometimes it was best to leave things be, and just concentrate on the future, but I felt certain that the situation with Bailey wasn't one of them.

We both looked down at the poster I was making. The color photograph of Bailey looked stark against the white background. The light was harsh, and every jagged rib, every bone on the dog's body could be seen. Every sore, every patch of missing fur. He looked a real sight, and I hoped the harrowing image would impel people to release information if they had it. The poster headline read: DO YOU KNOW THIS DOG? Underneath it I'd written the sanctuary details and phone number. It was now up to the volunteers to photocopy it and put the posters up around the town.

The next morning at tea break, around 10 a.m., the motley crew trooped in with their mugs of coffee and tea. I was leaving for the hospital in an hour to undergo my daily radiation therapy session as my appointments for this week were all in the afternoon. Apparently the consultant structured it that way to make it fairer for people who had to come long distances—like us.

I always sit in my chair at the back of the living room, with one or other of my dogs at my feet while the gang chats about the work they're doing on the site. I always tell them they can only come into my living room if they "behave" as my way of a jest, but there was no joking this morning.

"It's shocking. I've never seen a dog so thin," sighed Harry as he sat on the corner armchair, having trailed mud across my carpet from his boots.

"It's a disgrace. They should be prosecuted," said a young woman I didn't recognize. It was heartening to see so many young people who cared deeply about animals coming here and making a difference.

"If Barby's got anything to do about it, they will be," grinned Brenda as she marched in.

Brenda was a slight, fair-haired lady in her early sixties, who had once run a company and was now our redoubtable rehoming manager. No one messed with Brenda. She had a stern look over her glasses that froze anyone who dared challenge her.

"Well, you're right, because I've got these to put up around the town," I said, flourishing a bundle of posters in my hand. "Here you go, Harry, give these out to everyone, and make sure they put them up all over the place. I want the culprits found."

Harry took them from me and handed them out. There were murmurs from those who hadn't yet seen Bailey in the flesh.

"I can't believe it," gasped one.

"What bastards did this?" said another.

Just then Fran walked past my window, heading for the bungalow. He sidled in through the door.

"I've had an idea," he announced, looking straight at me.

"Well, there's always a first time," I deadpanned.

At that moment Di also came in. "Be nice to the old battle-axe, or she'll go for you," she laughed, winking at me.

Fran, who was used to my feisty spirit, ignored me and Di completely and continued: "I'm going to look into greyhound rescue charities. There are a few places that take in unwanted or abandoned racing greyhounds once their days on the track are over. I wonder if they'll recognize him."

"That's a good idea, Fran. Well done," I said, meaning it. As much as I liked to wind him up sometimes, he was always so thoroughly unperturbed by any banter. Aside from my digs, it was sobering to see how many people at the sanctuary had been affected by Bailey's arrival. The sense of shock was palpable in the fact that people could talk of little else.

After tea, I headed down to the kennels. It was my turn to take over from Christine for the next hour, and I wanted to keep a close eye on Bailey until it was time for me to leave.

Even walking across the yard left me breathless these days. It was taking me months to get over the physical effects of the surgery, let alone each day's radiation therapy.

I was sixty-eight when I was first told I had a malignant tumor in my left breast. I'd not wanted to go to the routine mammogram in the first place, but Christine had insisted I go. She had dealt with people dying of cancer every day when she was an end-of-life nurse at a local hospice, and she'd practically ordered me into her car before driving me down there. I got the results a few weeks later in the form of a letter calling me back for a biopsy and another mammogram. When I entered the prefab building and saw the room filled with silent women, each clutching their letter, all waiting for the bad news that was sure to come, I realized that this was real, and it might well be very serious indeed.

The biopsy was taken, and the results were given to me that day by my consultant.

"You have cancer, Miss Keel," he said, staring at me through his glasses, a look that wasn't without compassion. I had never thought I'd hear those words. I had always been fit and healthy: looking after my animals, carrying bales of hay, lugging round big sacks of goat pellets or horse feed come rain or shine, frost or heatwave. Never for a moment did I think I'd ever be taken ill. It had been a huge wake-up call.

Then to have another tumor in the same place only five years later! Perhaps it was my fault for choosing not to have chemotherapy? Who could tell? I had to face those same questions all over again: *Would I die? If I died, who would look after Gabby and Harry? Who would run the sanctuary? Who would raise the funds? Who would keep everything going for the charity?*

So many animals depended on me, even more so today than five years ago. Many a night I'd lie in bed sweating at the thought of my helplessness in the face of questions I simply couldn't answer. And it had happened again, though this time I'd known what lay ahead. I submitted as graciously as I could manage to yet more mammograms, a biopsy, and the dreadful news all over again. This time I'd reluctantly agreed to undergo radiation therapy as well as the surgery.

"You probably won't lose your hair, Miss Keel," my consultant, Dr. Allen at Brighton Hospital, had said to reassure me, "and it's very rare to get burned by the radiotherapy, very rare. There's really nothing for you to worry about, and the alternative is that if you don't do it, you risk the tumor coming back again."

I'd nodded in response. It made perfect sense. I'd risked its return once—and there I was, back in his consulting room, his computer turned away from me and my head spinning that I had cancer once again. Fortunately, my longtime friends Elaine and Rob were by my side in the consulting room. Elaine had given my hand a squeeze as if to say, "Well done, girl" for doing the right thing, but my heart had sunk. The shock of the diagnosis wasn't as bad as the first time I was told, when it felt like my whole world had collapsed around me. All the images I had of myself as being fit and well, capable and independent, dissolved away when I realized I would be needing all the help from others I could get. Elaine and Rob had been as amazing with me then as they were now. They took me to the hospital each time I needed to go. They were there when I woke up from the first bout of surgery, then again for the second.

When I came round from the anesthetic, my eyes flickered open to see sunlight streaming into the ward, making me blink. I had immediately felt a strange sensation of not being able to move, being held down by a weight, something that was hurting and sore. I had blinked again. My head was spinning and I felt distinctly woozy. I looked over to see the familiar machines at my side, the drip lines going into the cannulas on my arms, and at that moment I realized I'd survived the operation for the second time.

"Now then, Barby, don't try moving. You just lie still and let us take care of you," a kindly nurse had said to me. I hadn't realized she was in the ward next to me. I looked up at her.

"You're our special patient today, Barby. Everyone knows who you are and what you do for animals, so you're our ward hero." She smiled, adjusting the speed of the saline drip.

"That's very kind, dear. Well, I'm alive—that's good anyway," I had joked, then grimaced as I'd attempted to move my left side out of habit, leaning toward the nurse.

"What did I tell you, Barby?" she chuckled. "Stay as still as you can for now. This machine is for your morphine," she said, putting a small gadget in my hand. "You can click this button here every five minutes if you want to, it's important to keep on top of the pain. Don't let yourself get in too much discomfort. It's better to keep the levels of morphine in you steady, so no more heroics, please."

"Thank you, dear," I replied. My mouth felt dry. I clicked

the button, and a few seconds later I felt the warm rush of the medication hit me.

"I'll leave you for now, but if you need me, ring your buzzer. There, I'll put that beside you as well, and I'll come straight to you. Okay?"

"Okay," I'd said, as gratefully as I could manage.

I must have drifted off, as what seemed like a minute later, Elaine and Rob were at my side, both sucking on sherbet lemon sweets. Elaine was arranging a vase of flowers while Rob was working on a crossword puzzle.

"Welcome back, Barby. Bit of a déjà vu, isn't it?" said Elaine, grinning. "The good news is you can leave tomorrow morning if you behave yourself," she smiled.

"Oh, I can't do that, never have been able to do what I'm told. That's good news, though, better than last time anyway."

Luckily, this second operation had been keyhole surgery, so I had stitches rather than the twenty-six clips I'd been left with the first time. For that, at least, I had been grateful.

"How's Gabby, how's Harry? Did the guinea pigs come in yet? What has Dan done about that pig that needs rescuing?" As soon as the queasy postoperative feeling had passed, I immediately wanted to know what was happening at the sanctuary. Looking after animals was my life. In fact, I cared more for them than for myself.

"She's only been awake for an hour, and already she's trying to get back to work. Will you ever learn to retire and live peacefully?" Elaine had joked, knowing full well my answer to that would always be a resounding "No!"

"For a start, you've only been gone for a few hours, and you'll be back tomorrow so all that can wait," Elaine told me firmly.

"Gabby is being looked after by Diane, and so is Harry. They are perfectly fine. What's important is that you rest and make sure you get back to bossing us all about by tomorrow. Deal?"

"Deal," I had grumbled, which made both Elaine and Rob burst out laughing. They stayed all afternoon until visiting hours ended.

"We'll be back tomorrow lunchtime to see how you are, and take you home if you're allowed," Elaine said, waving as they both left.

"Don't you worry, I'll be ready," I replied.

Already I'd reduced the number of clicks I made on the morphine machine. I didn't like the feeling it gave me, a fuzzy head, nausea, and a dry mouth. I would much rather have just dealt with the pain in my own way, by grinning and bearing it, and so that's what I decided to do.

Once my friends had left, calm settled on the ward. The last rays of August sun faded from the sky, leaving a glorious burnt-orange cloud formation and the promise of yet more warmth to come.

The next day, my friends were as good as their word. They appeared in the afternoon to take me home, and came in to see me each morning to check on me and make my breakfast. I couldn't have asked for better friends.

I'd met Elaine and Rob in 2001 when they had arrived at the sanctuary asking if they could volunteer. They'd been sit-

ting out in their car for a while before coming in, and me
being the stroppy old woman I am, I had marched out to see
what they were doing. When they told me they wanted to become volunteers, I invited them in for tea and that was that.
We became firm friends, and Elaine, a diminutive woman
with a short blonde bob and able manner, started work in the
shop when it opened, and Rob, a sprightly, caring man, had
joined her in doing whatever he could around the site. They
were both as dotty about animals as I was.

Over the years, I'd often complained to anyone who would
listen that I should never have gone for that routine mammogram in the first place, and I would never have known about
the cancer, and perhaps that would've been better. Who could
tell? I'd read reports about elderly women not having surgery
because the tumors grew more slowly as they grew older, but
I didn't know if there was any rational sense in those stories.

As I went outside to check on Bailey, I gasped as the cold
air made the pain in my side throb. The sky was a thick gray,
and it looked like it would rain again. Winter had most definitely arrived. Each morning the cockerels would resist
crowing until 6 a.m. at the earliest, whereas in the spring
and summer they'd be awake from 4 a.m., sometimes earlier.
The sheep and goats stayed huddled in their pens all day,
their wool, ears, or horns showing above the mound of hay
they snuggled into. The trees that covered the site had all lost
their brown leaves and were standing resolute, their naked
branches crisscrossing the sky. I sighed. It felt like it would
be a long, cold winter ahead, and we had so much work to do
with this greyhound.

I entered the kennels quietly. Bailey's ears twitched at every noise, especially at footsteps, I'd noticed. Gently I sat down next to him, stroking his ears. "You must have been so scared of those people you lived with. You jump at every noise, every movement. . . . So what are we going to do with you, gorgeous boy?" I said, as much to myself as to him.

Christine appeared with a cup of tea for me, which I gratefully took in my freezing-cold hands.

"He's still too weak to walk, but he can stand, and he's responding to the medicine by eating tiny morsels of food but more regularly now. Already he's eating double what he was when he first came in, but that's not saying much," she sighed, her voice filled with sadness.

"There, there, boy, there's nothing to fear anymore. We're your owners, for the time being anyway, and we won't let anything bad happen to you ever again," I felt compelled to say.

Bailey turned his head to gaze at me. Again, that quiet spirit inside him reached out to me with a kind of agonizing tenderness. I couldn't imagine how anyone could look at his sweet angular gray face and want to hurt him in any way. But they had. That was the harsh truth. And now we were picking up the pieces, trying to fix a dog so broken he was barely able to walk.

"Come on then, let's have another teaspoon of this lovely food," coaxed Christine, holding it out to him.

"Let me," I said, taking the spoon, and holding it to his mouth. Bailey licked his lips. His ears twitched forward, and he licked it once, then again, taking a little sustenance at least.

"Well done, what a good boy you are," I exclaimed, feeling

genuinely moved by his gesture. He sank his head down again, panting now from the effort of moving. My heart squeezed tightly. I was not going to let this beautiful creature die. I was going to make sure he lived and thrived if it was the last thing I ever did.

"He's so scared of everything. When some of the last leaves on the ash tree fell beside his run, he was so startled," Christine told me. "It's so upsetting when something as innocuous as a leaf frightens an animal. It means there must have been terrible violence in his life to be so timid." We both fell silent at that. I could only imagine the horrors that lay in his past.

For hours we both sat with him. Most of the rest of that day was spent stroking his bony body and trying to soothe him, both of us desperate to keep him alive at all costs. With so much muscle wastage and body-fat loss, his prognosis was still touch and go. When a dog has been starved, its metabolic rate slows down to keep the body working—the body goes into survival mode and burns ketones in order to keep the organs functioning. It is very dangerous to then overfeed a starved dog, as the overload of carbohydrates can cause seizures, muscle cramps, and weakness, even respiratory failure. It is a balancing act between feeding the animal enough so it survives, and possibly causing more problems, some of them serious, if it isn't done correctly. We'd unfortunately had lots of experience in dealing with emaciated animals, though none as bad as Bailey.

"We'll get there, Barby, I know we will," Christine said.

"He is desperate to be loved."

As if in response, Bailey wagged his tail.

Chapter 7

KEEP GOING

I hadn't slept at all the night before due to the effects of my latest radiation therapy session. It was remarkable how a two-minute procedure with high-tech equipment could leave me so drained the following day, as if I'd run a marathon.

Thankfully I'd learned that I would be given three weeks' reprieve over Christmas and New Year as the department would be shut to all except the most urgent of cases. At first I'd been nervous about the treatment, having seen a friend go through chemotherapy years ago. She had suffered badly from the side effects of the chemo, and even though my consultant had reassured me that radiation therapy was much kinder to the body, I wasn't completely convinced, especially as I'd been feeling so sore since beginning the treatment.

Elaine had chatted all the way to Brighton while Rob drove, but I couldn't take my mind off the greyhound lying in my kennels. My worries about the radiation therapy seemed to melt away.

"You okay, Barby?" Elaine asked, kindly.

"I know I should be worrying about myself and this bloody radio-wotsit-therapy, but I can't help thinking about Bailey. Since he arrived a week ago, I can't think of anything else," I replied.

I watched the familiar houses and roads flash by, but all I could see was the frail greyhound lying with his head on Christine's lap.

"I don't know how anyone could be so cruel. I just don't understand," Elaine sighed, shaking her head.

Rob murmured his agreement. "But, Barby, it's time for you to look after yourself. This radiation therapy isn't a walk in the park."

I knew my friend was right, but the sight of Bailey staggering around my yard would haunt me for a long time to come. Every time I closed my eyes, he was there, gaunt and afraid. I'd still not slept properly since he'd arrived, and when I did, my dreams were full of harsh beatings, of heavy footsteps and a sense of overwhelming foreboding.

We'd also had no news yet from the public even though posters had been put up everywhere. Several volunteers at the sanctuary had reported that there were rumors in town that Bailey had been owned by travelers who had simply pulled up stakes and left, but whether that was true or not, it was hard to tell. We knew from the welts and sores around his neck that Bailey had spent a lot of time chained up, and there were urine scalds on his skin from being too weak to move away from where he was chained to do his business. The thought made me feel a mixture of nausea and fury. He was covered in fleas from sleeping outside and mange from the mites that foxes carry.

"We're here," Elaine announced, bringing me out of my dark thoughts. But even as we walked through the hospital wing and into the radiation therapy area, my mind returned to Bailey. I hadn't had time to check on him before we left because I'd had pressing issues with the Christmas Bazaar to deal with that morning, but even so, I wished I'd snuck out to the kennels before daybreak to see him, just to reassure myself he was alive, and if not well, then at least recovering.

"Barby, they'll ring you if there's a problem with the dog," Elaine said, patting my hand.

I wasn't so sure. Perhaps no one would dare call me just before my treatment. Perhaps they'd think I was too ill or vulnerable to give me any bad news. I had to hope that Elaine was right.

I undressed and put on the hospital gown that gaped at the back. I lay down on the radiation therapy bed and waited as the machine whirred into action and was positioned correctly over the exact spot where the tumor had been. Then two seconds later, it was over, and I had barely noticed. I always joked with my friends that it took longer to get undressed than it did to have the therapy.

It wasn't until we were back in the car and heading home that I started to feel the dead weight of tiredness slug me again. The same had happened after all the other treatments, and I never really had time in between each session to recover from it, so I was still far from my normal fitness levels.

Arriving home, all I could think about was lying down for a few hours' rest.

"Barby, we've got news about Bailey," Fran called across the yard as I walked slowly back up to the house. Elaine and Rob had stayed with me to make sure I got in and settled, and the three of us immediately turned to him. Fran had a cap pulled over his head and was texting rapidly.

"The greyhound charity got back to us," he explained, putting his phone away and striding over to greet us.

"Let me get inside, then tell me everything. Elaine, would you mind taking my bag, dearest?" I smiled.

Any news was good news. Any information we discovered about the dog in our care could be helpful in his recovery. The more information and detail we had about an animal's past experiences, the better; it helped us to learn what triggers the dog might have for disruptive or antisocial behavior, not that Bailey had exhibited anything like that in his time with us.

Fostering animals is a difficult task. Very often, and especially when an animal has been dumped or abandoned, we know very little about their background, what they like or dislike, how they've been treated, and whether or not they've been trained or cared for properly at any point in their lives.

These days, with more and more creatures being thrown out like the rubbish, we saw animals whose medical history and behavioral issues were completely unknown to us. It was like trying to complete a jigsaw puzzle with half the pieces missing. Without any background information, we were often working in the dark, unable to ascertain if animals had been vaccinated or even given basic training. It made our job harder—and it meant that animals had to be kept with us for longer so that we could carry out all the necessary checks.

"Go on then, Fran," I said, once I'd settled into my favorite armchair. Elaine fussed around me, bringing tea and a cookie, though I was feeling faint and sick and really didn't want food at all. My head was banging with a headache, and the site of the treatment on my left breast was starting to feel sore again.

"Are you sure you're well enough to talk now, Barby? I can always come back later," Fran said, peering at me with concern.

"Thank you, dear. I'm fine. I want to know everything I can," I answered, mustering my strength and taking a sip of tea. It was piping hot and very sweet, but within seconds I felt a little revived, and I waved at Fran to go on.

"Well, I checked Bailey over and found a tattoo in his right ear. Every racing greyhound has one to identify them. It's a series of numbers and letters. Anyway, I got straight on to the charity and they were able to trace him. He was a racing greyhound, and it looks like he was bred to race, which means he would've started at a training kennel when he was about a year old, and when his confidence improved, he'd have been taken to the track a few times a week to train him up."

Fran, having once been an animal activist, was well informed about dogs used in sport, and his knowledge was invaluable, though he had given up hunt "sabbing" (being a saboteur) years before I met him.

Fran continued: "At around eighteen months of age he

would've been entered into preliminary races, then maiden races if he did well."

"How often would he have raced?" I asked, wondering what went wrong for Bailey. Racing owners only retired their greyhounds to charities like the one that had taken Bailey in if the dogs performed badly, had become sick, or had been injured on the track. There were no obvious injury scars, like a badly broken leg, for example, that suggested that this had happened. Perhaps Bailey had simply lost too many races or fallen ill, which often happened as greyhounds are rarely kept in the best conditions.

"Probably twice a week, until he stopped winning or got injured. Who can say? The racing owners gave him to the charity. He wasn't there long before he was rehomed, but the charity couldn't give us any more details. The trail went cold after he left."

Disappointment hit me. "So we're really no closer to knowing who it was who treated him so badly."

Fran nodded.

At that moment, Elaine cut in. "And it's no use you fretting, Barby. You have to realize that the past is the past. Bailey is here now and getting the help he needs. You have to focus on that and not dwell on those people. Even if you did know who they were, what on earth could you do about it?"

Elaine was always right, but I refused to acknowledge it on this occasion.

"I'd bloody well go round there with a shotgun," I countered fiercely.

"Barby, you haven't got one, or at least I hope you haven't!" Elaine laughed but she looked directly at me, rather like my mother did when I was in one of my uncooperative moods as a child. It was the same stern expression, and I balked under it.

"Of course I haven't got a gun, but I'd blimmin' well find one. Perhaps you're right and it's best not to know." My headache was getting worse, and my left side was throbbing. I felt suddenly exhausted, not just from the treatment and re-sulting pain. Rescuing animals was at times a thankless and harrowing task. I'd never be able to hold those brutes account-able. A feeling of helplessness swept over me.

"Help me into my bed, will you, Elaine? I think I need to rest," I sighed.

"Right you are. Good decision. Now come on, old girl, let's get you in there. I'll stay to cook you some dinner—and no arguments, you have to eat something, Barby."

Elaine knew me so well. I was on the verge of arguing with her, telling her not to be so daft and to go home, that I was perfectly capable of looking after myself, but I knew I wasn't, and I didn't like the feeling one bit.

"Come on, Gabby. Come on, Harry. Elaine is in charge, and we're going to have a little sleep," I said to my hounds, dozing at my feet. I felt so lucky to have them by my side.

The next morning, I woke early after a fitful sleep and went straight out to Bailey. Christine had left in the early hours, and now there was no one there but me and him.

Bailey was lying on his side on the dog bed we'd made up

for him. His elegant head and long nose rose up as soon as I opened the door.

"Still skittish, eh, boy?" I said softly as I entered. I carefully knelt down next to him and stroked his ears. "So you were a racer, eh? Well, you're going to be a beautiful, spirited boy again one day. We'll see to that. I wonder why they stopped you from racing. Did you lose a race? Did you hurt yourself? Did the racers treat you well? We hear terrible stories here of greyhounds being kept in small filthy kennels and not being fed properly, but we'll never know what happened to you, will we . . ."

Bailey looked up at me as I spoke to him, just as if he understood every word. He licked my hand though he was trembling still.

"The sound of the wind outside is scaring you, isn't it? Oh you're such a poppet. How could they mistreat you?" Bailey's eyes were currents of sadness. I stroked his body, feeling each rib, each bone as my hand traced his thin frame.

"I know what it's like to be scared. When they first told me I had cancer, I went into complete shock. The room spun, the light became harsh, the words the consultant was saying just whirled around my head. And I was so frightened of the surgery, and whether I'd live to see another day. Well, I'd never thought about death, except to mourn the loss of my father and beloved brother, Peter. I'd never confronted my own mortality. It wouldn't happen to me, or that's how I be-haved. Silly really."

I talked to Bailey as if he was a close friend. He just watched me, occasionally sighing.

"You must've felt like that too when they left you cold and starving. Or when they hurt you. You must've been terrified of the pain and being threatened like that.

"I couldn't believe the agony I felt when I came round from that first surgery. When the nurse told me they'd put twenty-six clips into me rather than the six stitches and key-hole surgery I'd been promised, I felt real horror. I had depression after that. I just didn't see the point of going on, and I even wished I'd never had the cancer operation and thought I should've left it instead, though I might not have been here today with you, Bailey, and that wouldn't do, would it?

"I felt so low, so useless after my surgery, so weak and unable to do everything I normally could do around the site, that I thought of leaving the sanctuary. Can you imagine that? No, well, neither could I."

Bailey's tail wagged a little as I said this.

"Ha, I really do think you understand me a little, don't you, boy? Anyway, I hate hospitals now, and I'm going to do this blimmin' radiation therapy under duress."

At that point I leaned back against the wall. Today I felt tired and dizzy to the point of exhaustion. The sessions were starting to hit me hard, and I knew I wouldn't have the strength to carry out even the most basic of admin jobs today. Far better I was here, keeping Bailey company in the kennels on this chill winter morning until it was time for Elaine and Rob to collect me once again for that same trip back to Brighton. By now, we all knew practically every house, every tree, and every pothole on the way. Sitting here with the greyhound in the quietest part of the day was all I was fit for.

Bailey had settled down, but at each new sound, when the wind whistled or one of the volunteers called from another part of the site, he'd put his head up and scan the room, as if he was expecting danger to appear at any moment. Despite this, he was a very gentle dog, and had let us all touch him and stroke him, even though he'd suffered terrible abuse. He was plainly so desperate to be given affection that this overrode any fear of humans.

"But when the cancer came back a second time, it felt different. I wasn't as scared and was sure I would get through it as I'd done it before. You have to do the same, Bailey. You have to pull through. You have to keep going, just like I did. . . . Neither of us has any choice in the matter but at least we have each other."

Chapter 8

SCARS

The breaking dawn sky was dark, gray clouds hanging low, giving the morning an oppressive feeling. I shivered, despite being wrapped up in a winter coat, scarf, and heavy boots with thick woollen socks.

I was sitting with Bailey on his bed. I'd crept out before sunrise, leaving Gabby and Harry snoozing on my bed. I was still sleeping only fitfully, and so each day I woke before dawn after only a few short hours of broken sleep. The greyhound and the cancer treatment had shaken me up, reminding me of how fragile life really was, and yet every day this dog was showing me how resilient and strong we could be in the face of a myriad of horrors.

I wanted to show Bailey that there were people here to love him now. He had been with us for just over two weeks. I knew the transition from being in an abusive situation, suffering violence and starvation, to being a happy, healthy dog would take time, but I also knew the power of love when it came to animals and humans. With enough love, care, and patience, even the most damaged animal could, in their own time, be brought back to a place of healing. Sometimes it took months, as in Gabby's case, but sometimes it took just weeks or days. Bailey was already starting to eat well. He was taking sips of water constantly, and was wolfing down his small portions of Hill's Prescription Diet wet canine food, which was extremely encouraging.

He shifted next to me and I moved my fingers delicately across the scarring on Bailey's body. I could already see signs that he was starting to get better: there was already a more "solid" feel to him, and some of the sores were healing, though I knew they would take longer to mend than would be expected from a well-nourished dog.

"Look what they did to you. How could they?" I sighed, tracing the scars on his back with my fingers. Without thinking, I absent-mindedly felt along my own scarring left by this latest round of surgery, though it was swaddled under layers of clothing. I recalled the first time I looked in a mirror, not long after Elaine and Rob brought me home from the hospital after the operation at the end of August. I'd gathered my courage and, after undressing for a shower, probably the first I'd been allowed since the operation, I'd stood and looked at myself properly, without ducking away or turning off the light.

An old woman stared back at me, her face gaunt with deep black circles under her eyes and graying hair, though it was still streaked with blonde. It was in stark contrast to the image I remembered of myself as a young woman. Then I'd been known in Eastbourne as "the girl in the white bikini," because, every chance I got, I would go to the beach and sunbathe between shifts as a chambermaid at a local hotel. I teamed up with a friend who looked similar to me, and we'd let ourselves be chatted up by the sailors at the marina, and agree to meet up in a nightclub. We might have been approached by eight young men between us at different times of the day, and we'd tell them all to meet at the same time in the same place. What rotters we were. When the time came that evening, we'd hide outside the club and watch as each of the men arrived separately to meet the girls of their dreams. How we laughed, thinking of them waiting for us, perhaps making awkward conversation until they realized they were all there to meet the same girls.

How life had changed. The woman who stood before me had been through so much in her life: evacuation, seeing the impact of Luftwaffe bombing raids when her house had been struck and left in rubble, a difficult relationship with her mother, the deaths of her beloved father and brother, and many other challenges, not least of which was setting up an animal sanctuary with very little money and only my own formidable strength of will.

I expected to be revolted by my body, to feel it had betrayed me by producing the lumps that could've killed me, but instead I saw a resilient, hardworking fighter, a woman who cared little for how she looked anymore. After all, the animals didn't care whether I had scars or not, had gray hair or not, had wrinkles or not, so why should I? My body was changed forever, though, just as Bailey's probably was.

When an animal has been as severely neglected as Bailey had, it has long-lasting consequences. The immune system would be extremely hard hit, and this often causes other infections and illnesses that are hard to treat due to long-term malnourishment. The process of nursing a starved creature was painstakingly slow, and it had to be that way to avoid any complications with their already depleted system. Vomiting and diarrhea were common in recovering animals as their stomachs adjusted to the new feeding regime, or to having a feeding regime at all.

The effects of the neglect and violence upon Bailey were not just physical. In a way, the physical injuries were the easiest to treat, whereas the mental and emotional effects of psychological suffering were harder to heal, and more difficult to detect and cure.

Bailey had fortunately not become an aggressive dog, like many who are abused. He had obviously been socially isolated as he seemed unsure and afraid of human contact, and shied away from the other dogs in the kennel, but even that was already getting better, the more time we sat with him. He had been deprived of love for so long that he now seemed to want it desperately, and as a result hadn't displayed any antisocial behavior at all.

However, Bailey was withdrawing into himself, and this was as much of a worry as the opposite reaction of becoming vicious. Bailey was showing little interest in his surroundings and hadn't shown any willingness to play or sniff around, although he could still only manage a few short steps before flopping down, exhausted.

"You've got a long way to go, boy, and we'll be with you every step of the way," I told him, not for the first time. It was important for me to keep reassuring him, especially as he was starting to display some separation anxiety, another reaction to being isolated or kept away from people or other animals. He wanted to latch on to me, or Christine, and would pine for us if we left the room. The sound of his low moans was heartrending, but he had to learn to trust people again, and so it was important that he learned that if we left, we would come back.

Bailey's recovery was one of baby steps. He had to be rehabilitated back into the loving world of caring dog owners, and it occurred to me suddenly that perhaps he'd never experienced being loved at all.

"If you were bred to race and kept in the kennels, then perhaps you've never been shown proper, unconditional affection," I said out loud to him.

Bailey put his head to one side and wagged his tail a little.

"Yes, that's it. You've never been loved as you should've been. You might have been adored for winning, but you may not have ever been accepted for the lovely, gentle dog you are. Oh poppet, that is so sad." I felt tears well up in my eyes.

Stop that, Barby, I said to myself, crossly. I generally hated displays of emotion, but something in Bailey's story had struck a chord deep within me. Perhaps it was because I felt that I had never been loved truly for myself, by my mother, because I could never do anything right as a child. Perhaps it was because my mother had never cuddled me, not ever. As far as Mum was concerned, it was Peter who deserved her love, her cuddles, and her soft words. In response I became grumpier and more of a nuisance, sticking my tongue out at her, ignoring her commands, and generally behaving like a right little madam. I was ugly as a child: I had brown hair and a screwed-up face and was generally beset by the "grumps," as Dad called them. Peter was blond, blue-eyed, and had as sunny a disposition as you could imagine, but I couldn't ever hate him for it. I loved him with the same fervor as my mother, and my relationship with him was the big consolation of my childhood.

I don't think a child ever gets over knowing they haven't been properly loved. More often than not I was rebuked harshly by our mother. She never kissed me or cuddled me. She kept me fed, watered, and clothed but she never showed me any real affection. That I got from my father, and I was happy enough, but looking back, as I so often seemed to do these days, I realized that I had suffered neglect, and I knew how it felt, and how this poor dog beside me was feeling now.

"We've both been through a lot, you and me, Bailey. My life hasn't been easy either, and I've had too much time between the operation and now to think about it all. It isn't good to spend too much time dwelling on the past, Bailey, as it can haunt you forever."

Bailey moved, pulling himself up onto his legs, which quivered from the exertion.

"Steady, boy, take it easy," I murmured, although I was delighted to see him stand up and claim his space in his elegant way. He turned and sank down again, a small sigh escaping from his mouth, and he placed his head on my legs. I felt the thrill of connection with this creature. Delighted, I softly stroked his head and neck as I continued. He seemed to like listening to me ramble on about my life, and I was happy to talk. I felt we were drawn together, both of us having been through the flames and come out alive, but scorched.

Bailey looked up at me. His black eyes were full of sorrow, but there was also an innate wisdom there. For a moment, I thought, probably fancifully, that he understood every word, and somehow I felt that he sympathized.

"Dogs can read us humans, they know our feelings because they have them too," I said, smiling down sadly at the stricken animal.

Just then the door swung open and Fran appeared, dressed in his large dark woollen coat and muddy boots. The other dogs in the kennels began to bark insistently, making Bailey's ears flatten against his head and his limbs tremble even more.

"It's okay, darling, it's just Fran arriving to feed everyone. As soon as he gets here, the doggies all know it's breakfast time, and by now they're ravenously hungry," I soothed.

"Is that the time?" I exclaimed, looking at my watch. It was just past 8 a.m., and the day had started. Elaine and Rob would be here soon to collect me, as my appointments were scheduled for the mornings this week. I could hear the gate opening and the sound of other footsteps as volunteers arrived to start work. Someone called over to another, remarking at the cold. I'd forgotten how chilly it was and shivered when I heard them. The cockerels had started crowing about an hour ago, a sound that made Bailey jump a few times until I calmed him down, telling him they were silly creatures and they never knew what time it was.

"In the summer they start at 4 a.m., so we've had a lie-in, dearest," I giggled to myself. It was true. Those damn cocks were up before the crack of dawn, and they made sure the rest of us were as well.

"Now that Fran's here, you can have your next feed. We can't just let you eat whenever you want, though you probably feel hungry all the time now that you're having a regular food intake. We don't want that tummy to become more poorly, do we?"

"What are you doing here, Barby?" Fran asked, stomping his boots on the mat at the doorway. Without waiting for an answer, he started opening cupboards and bringing out various food and water bowls. I was pleased to see that Fran, instead of ladling some of the dog food onto a spoon, was instead dishing out a small portion for Bailey to eat from his bowl. It was the first "proper" meal the dog had been offered, having only been spoon-fed since his arrival. I was keen to see if he could manage a slightly larger quantity of food.

"Morning, Bailey. Here you go, boy," Fran said, gently patting the dog, whose head was still resting gently on my lap, and placing the bowl on the floor.

I moved away to give Bailey some space and was encouraged to see him sniff the edge of the plate and lick the meat juices hungrily. Soon he was wolfing down the portion, which must have been only a tablespoon of wet food in size at most, but it was a significant step forward for him. If he could keep it down, that was.

"Have you been here all night?" Fran asked, frowning, once Bailey had finished eating and was licking the empty bowl.

Obviously they'd all decided I was still too decrepit to look after the hound in any meaningful way.

"No, I haven't," I said, snappily. I hadn't intended to get cross, but I suddenly felt rather old and feeble. I'd only been with the dog for a couple of hours, but I felt cold and stiff, and knew it would be time for me to go. How frustrating this damn illness was. I'd much rather be mucking out the goats or pigs than creeping back to rest for half an hour in my arm-chair before my friends collected me, but my body gave me little choice in the matter.

"You look pale, Barby. You know you're not meant to be here. Christine and I have got it covered. She only went home a bit early last night because she hadn't slept properly for days. Bailey's fine, he's really responding to the food and the medicine Stephen gave him. Honestly, you should go and rest, you'll be much more use to us if you can get your head down."

I scowled at that, and tried to ignore him, instead petting Bailey to show him what a good boy he'd been in eating all of his food.

"I don't feel like I'm useful at all at the moment," I said eventually. "Diane and Brenda are refusing to let me help with the rehoming, Dan keeps insisting I sit in my sunroom and watch everyone else at work, and now you're telling me to 'rest' like I'm an invalid."

I knew I was getting emotional, but I couldn't stop myself.

"You *are* an invalid!" Fran exclaimed, chuckling to himself. Well, I couldn't argue with that.

In the silence that followed, Fran gathered the empty bowls

and, whistling, made his way into the rest of the building to feed the six other dogs currently housed here. All of them had sad stories to tell. There was Jack, a Staffordshire terrier, whose owners had almost been forced out of their rented accommodation, being asked to choose between their home and their dog. There was Ruby, another Staffie, who had been dumped on the roadside and found by a passerby who brought her straight to us. There was a mongrel called Denny whose owners simply couldn't afford their vet bills any longer. There were many other dogs brought to us who simply hadn't been wanted anymore. Another Staffie, Toby, had been abandoned because the owner's partner had gotten pregnant, as if a baby stops you from keeping a dog! Some of the stories saddened me, some enraged me, but I never communicated that to whoever was leaving their dog. Lives were complex, and giving up an animal was still a hard decision even if they'd simply got fed up with them. Dogs needed responsible owners who would commit to caring for them, and sometimes people's circumstances changed and the commitment could no longer be given.

As a young woman, I knew I didn't want children of my own. Perhaps it was because of my troubled and stormy relationship with my mother, or perhaps I was born that way. My mother ruled over me. I wasn't allowed to wear lipstick even at the age of eighteen, and I had to be home by 9:30 p.m. every night. She was controlling, and I think it put me off motherhood. The closest I ever came was a pregnancy scare when I was in my twenties. I was seeing an SAS bloke called Freddie. He was a bit nutty, probably not the best father material as he ate razor blades as a party trick. We met through a friend, and nothing came of it. I've never felt the urge to become a mother, though many of my friends became parents. I'd always assumed I couldn't have children, and perhaps that was true, though I never bothered to find out officially. My animals were my children, and I preferred it that way. Animals always gave so much back, they were uncomplicated, and in all the years I had run the sanctuary, I never once regretted staying childless.

"Go, Barby!" Fran interrupted my thoughts. I sighed again, somewhat theatrically.

"All right, I'm off. Goodbye, my poppet. You tell Fran to look after you properly, and if he doesn't he'll have me to contend with," I murmured to Bailey, stroking his dark head one last time. Fran only raised his eyebrows.

I got up, and, as I did so, Bailey looked over at me. His eyes met mine for a brief second of mutual understanding, before Fran marched over to check him over and begin the main business of the day, bringing him back to health, slowly and patiently.

Chapter 9

MOVING FORWARD

The door to the kennels slammed shut behind me in the wind. Bailey leaped up, his eyes wide with fear, every sinew straining, his senses on high alert. I don't think I'd ever seen an animal move so fast.

"Sorry, my darling, it's only me, sorry to startle you. . . . Oh dear, what will we do with you?" I hushed.

Bailey had been with us for three weeks now, and despite the hours of loving care, the stroking and gentle petting, he was still terrified by the slightest noise. I knew that the trauma he had suffered would take a lot longer to heal; it could take years, in fact, but despite this, I felt a little dispirited, wishing I could magic away his fears and help him to become what he was underneath all the effects of that cruelty: a happy, normal, loving dog. Every time he jumped, my heart sank. How could we help him to let go of that terror? It was a question with no obvious answer, except to carry on with what we were doing, and hope that, in time, his emotional wounds would heal as beautifully as his physical ones.

There are methods we employ when dealing with a dog that has suffered abuse or trauma. It is always important to let the dog come to us—rather than trying to force it into making contact. Any pressure on a vulnerable animal always backfires, and could result in aggressive or withdrawn behavior, exacerbating their psychological injuries. With Bailey, from the start we had made sure someone was always with him, sitting quietly and seeing if he wanted to snuggle up closer or be petted in his own time. It was an important part of building up trust with an animal. Showing gentle care and small acts of love, little strokes, and a soft tickle under the ear was better than overwhelming the creature with love and affection. Sadly, many animals weren't used to receiving love, and so it confused and startled them if it was too much too soon.

Obviously we followed the vet's protocol regarding food, water, and the beginnings of gentle exercise, knowing it was important to go at the animal's pace. Trying to speed up the recovery would be counterproductive, and we could all see that Bailey was too fragile to push any harder than we were. We would always give him plenty of reassurance when he was afraid and always communicated with him clearly so the boundaries were in place and his confusion could start to dissipate.

Building an animal's confidence is a key part of the recovery process, so I'd started taking Bailey for little hobbles around the kennel yard, making sure that with each circuit completed, he earned extra praise.

"Come and sit with me, come on now, boy . . . that's it,

come and have a little cuddle with me before the vet arrives,"
I said to Bailey, holding out a small biscuit for him to crunch.

Bailey had done so well on the special diet prescribed for
him by the vet that we were able to start giving him little dry
treats to supplement the wet food he was able to eat. We
couldn't overfeed him these, but it was a start, and it was
good to see him lick his lips and nudge my hand with his nose
for another.

"Greedy guts. Sorry, I can't give you another biscuit yet—
let's see how your tummy is with that one, and we'll go from
there. How does that sound?" I said, gliding my hand along
the length of his body. He still had dandruff and flaky skin,
a classic sign of malnutrition, and I'd noticed one day as he
went slowly outside to do his business that he was walking
strangely.

"It's like he's on tiptoes, I can't think of another way to
describe it," I'd said to Diane a couple of days before. "It's
like he's limping but on all four paws. I'll have to speak to
Stephen about it as it's very pronounced."

Diane and I were sharing a quiet cuppa before the hordes
of volunteers descended for their afternoon break. It was always a good chance to talk things through privately, rather
than surrounded by the seven or eight people who would
traipse in here with their muddy wellies and chat loudly over
steaming-hot mugs of tea and coffee. I didn't mind them coming in. They needed to warm up as it was bitterly cold outside.
The winter had really set in now, and the trees were all bare,
bar the evergreens, yet the animals still needed to be cleaned
out, fed, and watered, whatever the weather.

"It might be because he was starved," suggested Di. She was a fount of knowledge—and always surprised me by how much she knew about animals and plants of all kinds.

"When their diet is insufficient to provide the proper nutrients, lots of strange things can happen, including sore feet, I believe. Something to do with a low level of zinc." She sipped her tea and looked over at me. We were sitting in our usual places in the living room: me in my battered old comfy armchair facing my cabinet filled with a glittering array of cups and trophies, the result of my passion for playing darts, and Di in the armchair next to the doorway. Before I had a chance to reply, the first volunteer, Harry, stuck his head round the door.

"All right if I come in?" he asked before shooting me a cheeky grin and ambling in to take *his* regular place in the armchair by the sunroom.

Soon he was followed by an assortment of others, some of whom I hadn't met before. Brenda and Diane usually oversaw the volunteer schedule, and I was happy to delegate that responsibility to them. That day there were three youngsters, no older than their late teens, giggling together, their cell phones in their hands. The future of the sanctuary lay in the devotion shown by our young people, and I was heartily grateful for them being there. The December light was dim and gray, and even the slight shadows cast by the tree nearest Bailey's kennel had the power to unsettle him. He looked over at the tree swaying in the wind and whined again. So many things frightened him so we were all cautious when approaching him, trying not to make too much noise, and he had started to calm down more quickly. It was all moving in the right direction.

My strength was gradually returning, though the radiotherapy had hit me harder than I'd expected it to. Both Bailey and I were on the path to recovery, but it was a long, winding road, and as I stood there with him, fussing over him gently, I felt old and tired, both effects of the cancer diagnosis and treatment. Despite my exhaustion, I was determined that I wouldn't fail this animal as he had been failed so many times before. I knew it might take every reserve of energy I had to stay with him, keep feeding him, keep trying to walk him, and show him that his troubles were over and he was safe, perhaps for the first time in his life.

Bailey's still-emaciated body looked jagged in the gloom, though he had started to put on weight. He could now stand, which he'd struggled to do when he arrived, and he could gingerly take a few steps outside to do his business. It might not be fast-paced recovery, but it felt like a miracle nonetheless.

"Barby, Stephen is here." Fran poked his head round the door, grinning. "I thought I'd find you in here. He's starting to put on weight, I can feel it around his middle, and the sores are healing. I think the vet will be pleased with his progress."

"He's doing well, and he's such a lovely dog. Now, Bailey, the vet is here to see you again and so you need to be a good boy. Don't feel scared, he's here to help you . . ." I planted a kiss on the end of Bailey's long nose, which he accepted patiently.

"Hello, Barby. Goodness, is this the same dog?" Stephen appeared in the doorway wearing his customary white coat.

What I liked about Stephen was how he got straight down to business. His focus was always on the animal concerned; there was no need to chat about the weather.

"Yes, here he is. He's such a good boy. So gentle and peaceful. He's even had a few turns round the yard," I said proudly, like a mother showing off her child's achievements.

Stephen chuckled. He checked Bailey over, his face unreadable. He held the stethoscope to Bailey's heart and checked all down the length of his rib cage.

"Would you look at his paws, Stephen? He seems to be walking in an unusual way, like they hurt him."

"That's quite normal," said the vet, holding up a front paw. "Malnutrition does that. Keep feeding him up, little bits at a time, a few treats thrown in, and it should improve. If he's in real pain, then we can give him something. There, there, boy. You're doing well."

Stephen turned to me. "Well, Barby, you've done a great job in a short time. He's looking much better. The sores are healing nicely, and he's putting on weight, which are encouraging signs. His immune system will still be affected, so it's important to keep up the nutrition and lots of water. Has he been on any walks yet? Probably a good time to start him if not; perhaps try a small walk in the next few days. Don't overdo it obviously, but I think it'll do him good. You know where I am if you need me."

With that, he turned back to Bailey and patted his side, clearly impressed with the dog's survival instinct and resilience in the face of everything he'd experienced.

I needed to draw on Bailey's example to get through the

next few weeks. Christmas was fast approaching, and with the help of my staff I'd been able to stay away from the preparations for the bazaar as my radiation therapy had continued. It was usually held on a site away from the sanctuary, a fact I was very grateful for this year. At this time of year I'd normally be up to my neck in to-do lists and jobs to complete, but this year I did nothing. Even though I loved feeling useful, I also knew that I needed all my strength to get through the next few grueling months of radiation therapy. I had one more session to go before Christmas, after which I had a reprieve until mid-January. Elaine was busy at the shop and so it fell to Rob to drive me to Brighton Hospital. By now the parking lot attendant, the elderly man with the kind smile, recognized us and knew us both by name. Again, the actual procedure was entirely painless, but within a couple of hours I felt like I'd been hit by a truck. The drive back to Bexhill was a struggle for me. On top of the extreme exhaustion that followed each session, this time I felt a terrible burning pain around the scarring under my breast, far worse than the previous soreness. I said nothing to Rob as we drove, waiting until we got back to excuse myself straight away and head into the privacy of my own bathroom to inspect the increasingly painful area.

When I pulled up my sweater, I was shocked. The scars where the tumor had been removed were bright red, inflamed, and bleeding. The pain was now so intense I could hardly touch the site near the original wound. I let out a long, heavy sigh. Something wasn't right.

Despite my misgivings, I told everyone that I wanted to retire early, and they left me to it, thinking I was just very tired after the drive. I should have told them, but I have a stubborn streak that often finds me unable to ask for help. I was so used to doing things for myself, through being a self-contained person, a trait I probably had to cultivate in childhood because of my mother's neglect, and seventy years later it was almost impossible for me to change.

That night, I almost wept in pain. I didn't sleep a wink. Gabby sat with me for most of it. She knew I was suffering, and, in her own doggie way, she tried to help by not coming too close to me. Harry was stretched out on the floor fast asleep, dreaming of chasing rabbits in the field, no doubt.

"Oh Gabby, is this how poor Bailey felt when he was alone and in pain?" I asked her. Her beautiful honey face looked back at me, her eyes like melted pools of chocolate in the darkness.

"He suffered all by himself, never knowing when the next kick or cigarette burn would happen. He must have spent many lonely nights desperate for a little kindness or a salve for his wounds, or something to fill his belly."

My own pain only brought the greyhound's into sharper focus. Gabby put her head to one side, for all the world looking like she understood every word.

"He had it worse than me. He is the bravest dog I think I've ever known. He survived night after night of beatings. We know this because his wounds were all at various stages of healing—some wounds were older, some younger, so they must have come fairly regularly. And yet he still manages to be so gentle. I don't think I could be so forgiving," I said, my voice filled with emotion.

"I half expect you to reply when you look at me like that," I said, giving her a stroke, then wincing as a streak of red-hot pain ran across the area that had been seared.

"Oh dear, what have they done to me? That blasted consultant said I wouldn't get burned, and yet something has gone wrong. It can't be normal for it to be so painful." The night seemed to last forever. By the time the cockerels began their crowing, one starting then the rest following, tracing a circle of sound around the site, I was lying on my right side, trying not to cry.

"That's it, I'm calling the hospital as soon as I can," I said to myself, though Gabby bent her head and gave my nose a little lick.

"Was that a kiss to make me feel better? What a good girl you are." I managed a smile.

An hour or so later I was on the phone and managed to get through to the oncology department, where I was told rather brusquely that there were no appointments now until after Christmas.

"If you're in pain, then you must go to your GP or the ER. I'm so sorry but we can't help you. If you have any worries or concerns, you need to speak to your doctor," the not unkind but firm voice said at the other end of the line.

"That's what I'm bloody trying to do!" I said, exasperated. After taking some painkillers, something I have always been reluctant to do, the pain eased, and so I decided not to make a fuss so close to Christmas Day but to wait and see my consultant afterward.

"He'll get a piece of my mind, I can tell you," I grumbled

when I was back in the kennels with Bailey. "We're survivors, you and me, but it hasn't been easy for either of us," I sighed as he stared back at me, his face alert, his eyes full of intelligence as they returned my gaze.

"You're willing me to make it as much as I am willing you, I know you are," I murmured to him. Bailey stared back then dropped his head, snuffled and let out an extended sigh. I knew how he felt.

"It's Christmas Day tomorrow. No, it doesn't mean anything to me either," I said as Bailey wagged his tail a little and lay back down on his bed. "Ever since my dad and Peter died, I haven't had the heart to celebrate, though I will come and see you, don't you worry. Each year I do everything I have to do for the animals in the morning, and then come 2 p.m., I put a sign up saying 'Closed' and I retire to my living room with a ready meal, yes really, and a glass of sherry. I snuggle up in my blankets and watch television for the rest of the day. In the evening I light two candles, one for Dad and one for my brother. That's it. It's a simple day, and one I generally dread because it reminds me of the people I've lost."

I was silent for a moment after that. Outside I could hear Dan shouting to someone to bring some hay. The tractor was being revved, and the usual cacophony of sound from the geese, chickens, and ducks could be heard above it.

The next morning, I dragged myself out of bed at 6 a.m., determined to feed the gulls as usual, ignoring the fact it was a special day and intent on carrying on with life at the sanctuary in the only way I knew how. The pain had receded a little, but I'd still hardly slept a wink, and I had seen the big black bags under my eyes that seemed to be in permanent residency these days.

Diane stopped me as I made my way to the back to pick up one of the crates of broken-up bread.

"Oh no, you don't. I'm taking charge of feeding the birds now. You need to rest, and before you object I can see you're in pain. Barby, you're not Superwoman, though you like to behave like it. You need to rest, and it's Christmas Day, for heaven's sake," she chided.

"Oh, you know I don't like Christmas," I muttered, putting the heavy crate down. Secretly, I was relieved she'd taken charge as my left side was throbbing with pain, the burning sensation feeling intensely raw.

"From now on, I'll be doing the gulls each morning, and if I can't do it then Harry will. It's all decided," she countered, looking at me to make sure I'd heard her.

"Do you remember when we had two gulls to feed all those years ago?" Diane then asked, grabbing the crate.

"Yes, how could I forget? We had two gulls who we nick-named Pebbles and Elvis, and we used to go out with two slices of bread and feed them that," I replied, smiling at the recollection.

"Then there was Lurch as well. Three gulls with three slices of bread, and now we have three hundred!" Diane added.

At that we both looked round us. Gulls, crows, garden birds, and pigeons had started gathering, their wings beating against the overcast day, soaring on the winds that swept over the land. Their cries echoed down the valley, as Di started walking down to the point where she tipped out all of that food. Not a single bird tried to attack her or dive-bomb her for bread. They circled overhead, their wings flapping, and then they swooped. Diane stood back and grinned at the spectacle.

"Happy Christmas, dearest," she said.

"Happy Christmas—may it be a better year for all of us," I replied, "and especially for you, Bailey," I whispered, the wind tugging at my jacket.

Chapter 10

FIRST STEPS

"Exciting day, Barby!" Christine called out as she crossed the yard. "Do you think Bailey is ready for his first walk around the sanctuary?" She was swaddled in a thick fleece jacket, tough boots, and a scarf that wound almost round her face as well as her neck.

I was similarly attired. Both Di and Dan had told me in no uncertain terms to stay indoors because it was a bitterly cold January day, but I was undeterred. The pain in my left side had eased, and I'd been free of the radiation therapy for two weeks, so I was feeling a lot sprightlier.

"Well, let's see how he does, I don't want to push him too hard, but a walk is overdue. I should've taken him out after Christmas, but I didn't feel well enough," I called back, walking over to the door of the kennels, which Christine was now holding open for me.

"Are you sure you're up to this, old girl?" she joked kindly, looking me straight in the eyes with her honest gaze.

I paused for a moment, breathing in the sharp cold air,

filling my lungs with the goodness of it. "Yes, you know what, I think I am. I can't stand another moment being cooped up inside, and so it's better for my blood pressure that I'm out here with you."

Christine laughed at that. "Come on then or you'll freeze to death," she said, holding open the door and ushering me inside.

My staff weren't just people who did their jobs and went home. Perhaps because of the nature of their work here, the volunteers and workers were more like an extended family, all looking out for each other, and me. Like any family, there were sometimes conflicts or problems that arose between different personalities, but usually everyone rubbed along very well together. All of us were here because we had a passion for animals, and so it was the love of these abandoned creatures that drew us together, working for the good of the animals rather than any personal gain.

Christine, whose hair had darkened over the years from a honey blonde to a light brown, was a particular favorite of mine. She was always so reliable, so steady and incredibly caring. She wasn't a gossip. She worked hard, and she was utterly devoted to the dogs in her care. In short, she was very much my type of woman, and she'd become a close friend over the years. I knew she felt genuine affection toward me, as I did her, and it was a lovely start to the year to be out here, about to take Bailey for his first steps beyond the kennels, a fresh start for all of us, and a celebration of everything we'd both survived.

Even so, it was cold, and Christine pulled on thick woolly gloves before whistling gently to the dog. As soon as we'd arrived in the kennels, a chorus of barks greeted us, each dog thinking they would be fed or taken for a walk.

"Sorry everyone, we're here for Bailey this time. Poor pooches, you'd think they never got walked," I said with mock exasperation.

Each morning a team of volunteers arrived and took the dogs out, sometimes in pairs, but mostly separately. They'd navigate the lane before heading south into the fields that spanned our sanctuary. It was doggie heaven, there was so much to sniff, so many new scents to discover, and it cheered my heart seeing the dogs wagging their tails and trotting next to their walkers each day.

Today, it was my turn to walk our beloved greyhound. When Bailey saw us he got up and walked over, his tail wagging. He gave Christine's proffered hand an experimental sniff and came straight over to me. I crouched next to him, holding his head as I told him what a big day it was, for both of us.

"Today is the day we'll go out and show you this beautiful place, though mind you don't go upsetting the horses by barking as they'll show you what for. We're going to put a doggie coat on you now, as it's very chilly out there, and then we're going to see how far both of us can go. We'll be like two invalids walking together. Now, how does that sound—good?"

Bailey's eyes were calm and soft. He made a small whinnying sound in agreement, and licked my nose.

"That's enough of that, boy, I've already had a wash this

morning," I chuckled, stroking my hand down the bones of his back. "Now stand there like a good dog, and we'll put the coat on you."

Bailey was good as gold and didn't move a muscle while we wrapped his thin frame in a coat.

Outside, the morning had started with bright sunlight, and it promised to be a glorious, though freezing cold, winter's day.

"Shall we go?" Christine said, feeling in her pocket for treats and a leash. "Even though he's still pretty below par, I don't trust him with the chickens. It could reawaken his racing and hunting urges, and we don't want a poultry massacre on our hands," she added.

I nodded in response. Though Bailey was still very thin, he was clearly on the way to recovery as he'd put on some weight and was walking less carefully around the kennel yard, meaning the sores on his feet and legs were healing, giving him less pain. He'd had the best possible nutrition over the past few weeks, and so the possibility of him trying to pounce on our birdlife in the yard was definitely something to think about.

"Ready?" Christine said.

"Ready," I answered, taking hold of Bailey's leash. "Come on, boy, let's go and explore."

Bailey took his first steps out of the kennels with us beside him. I had worried that it was too soon, but I also knew I couldn't mollycoddle him forever.

"We are doing the right thing, aren't we, Christine?" I said as we crossed the yard. I trusted her advice, especially as she was as much of a dog lover to the core as I was.

"Of course we are. He has to start somewhere. We won't go too far, just a turn around the paddock and the back field, then back up to the house."

"Thank you, dear. I know I worry about him, but who could resist that beautiful face and gentle spirit?" I said, already feeling a little out of breath. "He's gorgeous, and it goes beyond anything I understand when it comes to how he was treated. We just have to do our very best to repair that damage, and that's exactly what we're doing."

Christine was a longtime volunteer at the sanctuary. She had started by walking the dogs once or twice a week but had soon become a regular. Away from the sanctuary she'd worked as an end-of-life nurse, and she used those skills when caring for mistreated dogs like Bailey. She was always unceasingly patient and kind, letting the dogs go at their own pace. I'd seen her spend many nights cuddled up with a traumatized animal, though mostly with Bailey, and each time I marveled at the wonderful kindness of some humans, while others would subject animals to unspeakable cruelty.

Once outside of the perimeter of the kennels, Bailey looked around him, seeming almost stunned by the views and change of scenery. His world had shrunk to the kennels and yard for the first few weeks of his rehabilitation, so it was no wonder that this strange new experience might overwhelm him a little. Also, as he was a track dog, I had no idea whether he'd ever experienced the great outdoors rather than just brief excursions onto the man-made track. He was used to crowds cheering and the noise of people betting on their races, but was he used to feeling the wind against his fur? Had he ever splashed his paws in fresh rainwater, run through long grass in the summer, or felt snowdrops land on his nose in winter? Bailey's background was largely a mystery to me, but my instinct told me that these simple pleasures had long been denied him.

His ears twitched at the icy air. He held his long neck and head up, smelling the scents carried on the breeze. He looked around him, blinking in the daylight. Just then Trousers, a daft chicken with extravagantly feathered legs that looked like he was wearing multicolored leggings, squawked past, breaking into a trot when he saw the greyhound. Bailey turned to look, and seemed to shrink back a little, scared at the sight of this bizarre creature. Trousers was known for being speedy, dashing across the yard at the merest hint of food, and Christine and I laughed at the sight of him.

"Don't worry, Bailey, he's just a silly creature. He won't hurt you."

We carried on, the other dogs in the kennels barking again as we passed on our way round the back of the work shed to the paddock. It was here that the untamed horses were kept. We had two mares in residence, both rescued from a farmer who had bought land only to find the two horses living practically wild upon it. Not knowing what to do with them, he'd called us, and Fran had been down to round them up, not a job I envied.

They were both swishing their long black tails, their nut-brown bodies glossy in the searing winter light. It was a perfect day to be out, but already both Bailey and I were struggling. We had reached the other side of the paddock when Bailey started becoming skittish. The horses had momentarily upset him, and in response, seeing us walking round their field, they had stopped cropping the grass and cantered to the back part of their enclosed space.

"Let's stop here for a minute, I'm all out of puff, and I think Bailey needs to settle down," I said, leaning on the wooden fence post. It was moments like this that I understood anew the blessing of living here, on this land, surrounded by startling natural beauty. The Sussex countryside stretched out behind us, with houses and farms dotted on the landscape. The fields of green and brown were cordoned off by fencing, but some areas stretched for miles. There were tree branches stretching into the sky and the distinctive smell of wood smoke from nearby properties. The sheer brilliance of the bare winter beauty took my breath away.

"It's incredible," Christine murmured, digging into her pocket and retrieving a treat for Bailey to munch on while they waited for me to catch my breath. Bailey had backed off when he saw the horses, which made me wonder if he'd been frightened by them in the past, though of course I would never know for sure.

"Sometimes I forget how lucky I am," I said, smiling over at her.

The wind tugged on my hair, making a few strands come free from my scarf. I pushed them back, squinting against the brightness. From nearby came the distinctive sound of a pea- cock, one of several we currently housed in the special pen which had now been finished. It was like a giant aviary, with chicken wire–style fencing arching over solid, tall wooden struts. It was one of the many improvements underway at the sanctuary, from new cement pathways between animal areas to the spruced-up kennels. There was always something to fix or update around the site.

"Let's get moving again, then, or we'll turn to ice out here," I rallied, setting off, with Bailey now following at my heels, round the side of the peacock pen and into the neighboring field, which was occupied by a flock of sheep, another rescue from a farmer who had sold his farm and relocated, leaving the sheep behind and no one, except us, to care for them. As soon as we entered the field and Bailey saw the flock, he stopped, sniffed the air, and looked up at me.

"It's okay, boy, there's nothing to fear. Let's keep walking. If any sheep come close, I'll shoo them away."

With that we set off again, but I was watching one particular sheep from the corner of my eye as we walked. Sid was a Jacob with a tendency to butt anyone who got too close. I saw him munching grass at the end of the field, and steered us left, round to the entrance to the second horse enclosure. Luckily we had five small ponies in there who completely ignored us as we ventured across their land.

"You okay, boy?" I said to the greyhound who was walking, albeit more slowly, by my side.

"I think he's gone as far as he's able to today," chipped in Christine.

"I know how he feels," I said, feeling suddenly breathless again. Perhaps I'd pushed us too hard. I knew that I was starting to feel a bit dizzy, let alone how Bailey must have been feeling, using his legs properly for the first time in goodness knew how long.

"Let's just say a quick hello to the pigs. Come on, Bailey, dear. Look, let me introduce you to Pinkie and Brains." Two fantastically ugly pigs lay bundled up in their straw, and so we were hardly able to see them beyond the tips of their upright ears. A grunt acknowledged our presence, but nothing further was forthcoming. Bailey looked unsure, and I realized it really was time to head back past the cattery and into the yard where the kennels were only a few yards away.

"Pinkie and Brains came here two years ago and were only supposed to be here for a short while, but the owners never did take them back," I said to myself as much as to anybody else.

It was a familiar story. Many people contacted the sanctuary, asking us to take their horse or pony, or even pigs, promising they would pay for their upkeep—and that would be the last we heard from them.

As we entered the yard, the geese and ducks scattered. The chickens stopped scratching the ground for grubs, and several of the feral cats that stayed with us overnight vanished as if by magic. Bailey seemed unaware of the effect his entrance had on the other residents. By now, his head was down and he was hobbling a little as his paws were still slightly sensitive.

A wave of pure anger swept over me—it was so powerful I had to stop.

"Everything okay, Barby? We're almost back," Christine said. She knew something wasn't right with me.

"I just can't bear what they did to him. Sometimes I look at him, how peaceful a soul he is, how loving and sweet his nature is, then I see how slow his progress is, and it's all too much for me. I hate those people who did this. I hate them. I know I shouldn't. I know it's better if I channel all my feelings into looking after him, but I can't help it." I was almost crying by now.

"Come on, Barby, you're tired too and you're still recovering. These walks will be as much for your health as for Bailey's. You both need some serious TLC, so get into the warm and we'll talk about it there." Christine's voice was firm.

Meekly I followed her in. I admit I felt exhausted by then. The cold had got into my bones, and yet my blood still boiled with anger on this dog's behalf. How could people do this to a defenseless creature?

It was a question without an answer.

Bailey seemed tired but content after his walk. Once we'd settled him down, and Christine had practically ordered me back to the bungalow, I took a hot cuppa into my bedroom and sat alone for a few minutes. I had to look after myself better, because how could I look after the animals if I wasn't okay? To that end, I picked up the phone and called the hospital, managing to get an appointment for the next week with my oncology nurse. Despite the fact my burned scar was feeling better, I still wanted answers. I'd also noticed that each time I brushed my hair, more and more strands of gray were collecting on the brush. I had wondered over the past two weeks if it was my imagination, but my hair seemed to be thinning, against all the advice I'd been given by the hospital before starting this treatment.

By the time I walked into my nurse's consulting room the following week, the pain and swelling had almost disappeared. When the nurse, a rather officious woman, said, "I wouldn't have bothered reporting that, it looks fine," I felt stung. My temper flared.

"Well, it's not surprising given that you wouldn't see me before Christmas. I was in agony, and the consultant told me I wouldn't get burned!"

I turned to Elaine, who was sitting right there beside me, expecting her to nod her head in sympathy. Instead she was grinning from ear to ear like a Cheshire cat.

"Well, your spirit is still there despite everything, Barby," she said.

I looked at her and suddenly let out a huge laugh. I turned back to the nurse: "And don't think I'm letting you off the hook, because I'm not."

Elaine was right. The weeks of debility and feeling useless had started to disappear. My old self was returning, and, in that moment, I fervently hoped that Bailey would feel the same too. It was time for both of us to live again.

Chapter 11

FEEDING UP

Feeding up a starved dog is never a straightforward process. It can be extremely dangerous to let an emaciated animal eat too much too quickly, causing catastrophic illness and even death, if not handled properly. When a thin animal comes into our sanctuary, the first thing we check for is any underlying illnesses or diseases that may be causing the weight loss. Dogs in particular often arrive riddled with worms, or may be suffering from eye or ear infections due to malnutrition, and other problems such as anal sores, tapeworm, and maggot infestations. The gums and tongue must be checked for anemia, which presents as a grayish color, as does rat poison ingestion. Water must be given straight away as dehydration is often a factor in these cases.

The right diet and medication are therefore vital for each individual dog, especially when lack of food or decent nutrition is part of the mix. A dog is considered to be emaciated if it has lost 10 percent or more of its body weight, according to breed or type as measured on the healthy-weight scale, a situation applicable to Bailey upon his arrival. The ribs and hip bones will be clearly visible, and the animal will appear to be "all skin-and-bones."

When a starved animal is presented, they should also be checked all over for microchips or any identification markers, such as Bailey's ear tattoo. This is in order to try to identify the animal—and its previous owners—plus any health issues it may have had in the past.

Once all of these problems, most commonly seen with stray, homeless, or mistreated dogs, are checked out and treated, the feeding must begin in very small steps. With Bailey it had been one teaspoon of prescription diet, high-nutrition food at a time, leading up to a tablespoon. By now, six weeks into Bailey's stay with us, I had started him on four small meals a day as he had gained some weight, and the risks associated with refeeding were now low.

Bailey seemed delighted to regularly receive his food in a bowl, and wolfed it down, looking up at me when he'd finished with an expression on his face that clearly said:

"And where's the rest, please?"

I smiled down at him. "What a good boy you are. You've eaten it all, but that's all I can give you—I don't want to upset your tummy. You can have another portion in a couple of hours' time."

Bailey cocked his head to one side, and gazed at me with that patient, abiding look of his. He really was a lovely dog. He was making slow but steady progress, and there wasn't a day that went by without me spending a few hours with him.

"You still here, Barby?" Fran said as he came through the door, stomping his feet with the cold.

"You can leave him with me now. I thought you had something urgent to do today?" Fran grinned.

I sighed in response. "I *always* have something urgent to do, didn't you know?" I complained with exaggerated exasperation. "Yes, I've got a Yorkie coming in today so I'd better be near the phone in case there's a hitch. Minnie the Mink's specially built shelter needs repair work, and there are a thousand and one things to do besides those."

I chuckled. Life was never boring here.

Minnie was our resident mink who had come into the sanctuary via stealth. I had ordered some wood chippings for one of the pens a year or so ago, and somehow Minnie arrived with them. At first she'd caused havoc, chasing the chickens around the yard before catching one and being grabbed by one of the volunteers as a result. The chicken was rescued, thank goodness, and Minnie was given her own pen with a run, her own little pool and a tree to climb, and, of course, daily food, which may have been difficult to hunt in the wild. Her home needed a few repairs after the winter, so I had to get someone to do that. Then the Yorkshire terrier was coming in, though at what time, I didn't know.

Whenever a Yorkie came into the sanctuary, I couldn't help but think of the 204 puppies we'd saved on Easter Monday in 2006. An anonymous tip led us to a shed used by breeders that was filled with animal boxes stuffed full of shredded paper—and the puppies. Dan had been one of the rescuers, and the sight that greeted him that day was indescribable. The puppies had been left to die. They were covered in their own excrement and urine, and they were ridden with fleas. There had been no light, no fresh air; they had been born to breed or die.

When Dan returned with eleven of the pups—the rest had been shared among other sanctuaries in Sussex—I couldn't believe my eyes. It was the most pitiful sight and has haunted me ever since. Filthy matted fur, foul stinking boxes, and twenty-two velvet-brown eyes looking up at me. My heart turned over at the sight of them.

"The smell was unbelievable," Dan had told me. "They had clearly never been cleaned. They didn't know what it was to go outside. They'd been left there to die. Then there were the dead puppies, just left there to rot among the living."

Once we'd cuddled them, despite their condition, and soothed them, I rang the vet and the dog groomers I always used. Some of the dogs tried to jump up to say hello but their legs were so weak they couldn't support their tiny bodies. Who knew how many other little souls had perished in those appalling conditions?

The next day the groomers arrived and spent twelve hours cleaning and de-matting their fur, leaving the dogs fragrant and ready to be rehomed.

I remember thinking that day that humans could be the cruelest animals of all. I turned back to Bailey, giving his side a rub and his ears a tickle. His tail wagged immediately. He was ever keen for loving attention, which I was more than happy to give him. Bailey had found a place in my heart, and I was starting to realize that it would be a wrench to ever say goodbye to him.

"Okay, Fran, I'd better go," I said gruffly, emotion welling up inside me.

Suddenly my walkie-talkie crackled and Di's voice sounded through it, making Bailey jump. His nerves were still jangly despite the weeks of care.

"Barby, can you hear me?" she said.

"Yes, dearest, go on," I replied, holding it up to my ear, and moving away from Bailey.

"Come over quickly, there's been a robbery." She sounded breathless.

"A robbery? What do you mean? What's happened?" I asked, already moving as fast as I was able toward the bungalow. I'd done most of the six-week radiation therapy course by now, the last session was only a few days away, and as usual I felt like I'd been hit repeatedly over the head and body with a blunt instrument.

"Just come now," was all Di said. I could tell by the urgent tone of her voice that this was serious. If I could have sprinted over, I would've, but the best I could do was walk a little faster. By the time I got to the living room and saw everyone standing around talking, their faces shocked and a feel of tension in the room, I was ready to drop.

"Oh here she is. Goodness, Barby, you look terrible. Sit yourself down, I'll get you some sweet tea, and we'll tell you everything."

Di took charge. She bustled into the kitchen and I heard the noise of the urn as it spat out boiling water. I was plonked into my chair and a cup of tea was placed in my hands, which I sipped gratefully.

"Tell me what's happened," I said simply.

Dan, Fran, and Harry stood close by, looking worried, and it was Dan who broke the silence. "The police just called. There's been a robbery at the shop in St. Leonards Road. Don't worry, the volunteers down there are unharmed, but they're shaken."

"Oh goodness," I breathed, "go on . . ."

"A couple of men had been browsing. Apparently they left, then came back when the till was open and demanded the money. Of course they just let them take it. It wasn't worth trying to stop them," he shook his head angrily, his usually kind face looking stern.

"How much did they take?" I asked, dreading the answer.

"Only £280, but it was everything in the till for that day," Dan sighed.

For a moment I was silent while I took in the news, and then I burst out, "It might only be £280, but that's a bag of animal feed we can't buy, a stack of wood we can't build fences with, a vet bill for the rabbits' claws we can't pay. How could they have been so bloody vile?"

I was furious. I knew that we were vulnerable to this type of thing as a charity, and both the staff down at the shop were elderly so were probably seen as "soft" targets—they must have been scared out of their wits. Didn't those brutes realize that this money was desperately needed for our animals?

Stealing was an ever-present problem at the shop. It beggared belief that people would rob from a charity, but they did and quite regularly.

I sighed, not for the first time that day, but this time it was infused with sorrow.

"Well, at least no one was hurt, that's the main thing. Okay, dears, thank you for telling me," I finished.

"Oh, and before I forget, Barby, did you hear that the Yorkie isn't coming in now? The owners have decided to keep him after all," sighed Di, as she pulled on her woolly hat and began making her way out of the door.

"Right you are. Thank you, dear."

It was at least one silver lining on a very dark day.

"Harry, while I think about it, would you go and fix Minnie's area? At least that's one thing we can get done today."

Harry had been a regular at the sanctuary for a few years now. He was tall and well-built, with dark hair, and he could often be seen pushing a wheelbarrow filled with cement or paving stones around the sanctuary.

There was no time to mope on this site. While I waited for the police to call, the money raised at the Christmas Bazaar needed to be allocated to various tasks, including renewing the Oldies pens and sheds (the name we gave to our elderly feline residents), refurbishing parts of the dog kennels, including the staff kitchen, and resurfacing the drives and walkways after the winter. There would be other animals coming in, and the phone, which rang constantly, needed to be an-swered.

Just then, on cue, the phone did indeed ring.

"Hello, Barby Keel, can I help you?"

"Hello, yes I hope so. We have ten hamsters that need to be rehomed," said a woman at the other end of the line.

"Ten? All right, dear, you'd better give me your details . . ."

Chapter 12

RUNNING FREE

It was the day before my last radiation therapy treatment, and I decided to celebrate by taking Bailey out for a longer walk this time, hoping that both of us would be up to the challenge of circumnavigating at least part of the site, if not the whole twelve acres.

Winter was still with us, though occasionally patches of blue appeared in the sky, a welcome reminder that spring was only a couple of months away. It had been drizzling overnight, so the ground was wet. Perhaps walking through wet grass would be another new experience for the greyhound?

Bailey bounded over to greet me when I arrived, another welcome sign, along with his growing appetite, that he was truly on the mend. When he'd first arrived, he had cowered a little in his bed, or sat quietly, taking everything, and everyone, in. Now he was very used to us, and he showed his delight in so many ways. Today his tail wagged excitedly as I patted his side and ruffled his short fur. I noted with pride that he definitely had meat on his bones now. He had filled out, and, although he was still way off the weight of a healthy grey-hound, it was progress nonetheless.

"Are we going walkies together, then?" I asked playfully, stooping to cup his beautiful dark-gray face in my hands and kissing his forehead.

At the sound of me saying "walkies," Bailey instantly responded, trotting over to the door and waiting patiently for his leash to be attached.

"Today I think I'll take you off the leash and let you run in our bottom field, though you have to promise not to run off and leave me," I said stoutly, still holding his aquiline features.

Bailey blinked back at me and licked my nose. That was good enough for me.

"Let's go then," I exclaimed, reaching for the leash and clicking it onto his collar.

Bailey was always good as gold. He never jumped up, which made putting his leash on much easier. He waited, like the gentle dog he was, and once the leash was on we set off together, this time taking the circular route past the cattery on the left and the FIV cat shelter on the right, through the farm-animal enclosure where Dan was hard at work feeding the pigs.

"Off for a walk, then, Barby?" he smiled, pushing back his curly dark bangs that had obscured his glasses.

"We are, Dan," I replied, "and look how well Bailey is doing now."

Dan grinned just as a huge great snout appeared over the fence. "He's a different dog from the one that arrived. Enjoy your walk," he said, "These pigs are hungry, so I'd better get on before they destroy their nice new pens."

I laughed at seeing the huge pink nose. I looked down to see what Bailey's reaction was to the snuffling, snorting pig waiting for his feed. Bailey had stopped and retreated a few steps.

"Come on, boy, those daft pigs are nothing to worry about," I said soothingly.

He looked at me in response, puzzled, and took a step forward to stand behind one of my legs.

"Oh dear, perhaps I've frightened you by taking you this way. I'm sorry, Bailey, but really, there's nothing to fear from the pigs. They're safely kept behind the fencing." I didn't add that, of course, if the pigs had wanted to get out they were more than capable of bashing down the fences, they were so big. But they didn't, because pigs are intelligent creatures who quickly learn they prefer having regular food and warm, clean bedding to running off into nowhere.

Bailey started walking again, but he veered over to my left side and wouldn't go any nearer to the pigs. We kept a steady pace as we walked through the pens and down through a small gate into the field where the sheep were kept. Again, Bailey stalled just as we entered, lifting his nose to smell the still-unfamiliar odor of the sheep and nearby goats.

"Come on, Bailey, you can do this . . ." I said as gently as I could manage, though I could feel mounting frustration. Had I pushed him too far too fast? Was this a crisis point for this poor dog? The point where Bailey retreated back into the frightened, beleaguered, cowering dog he was on his arrival?

Had I re-traumatized him by bringing him further out of his comfort zone?

I stood there, whispering to him, coaxing him to move, to remain by my side, not to feel afraid, and yet still he wouldn't budge. Just then, I remembered I had a dog treat in my pocket. I took it out. It seemed to break the spell. Bailey looked up at me and started to salivate. He shook his head, throwing off the panic that had overwhelmed him so quickly. I gave him the biscuit, and he crunched it and then nudged my hand for another. He had calmed almost instantly. I felt a rush of pride at this incredible animal. Even when something rattled his cage, he was able to bring himself back. What an extraordinary soul he was.

"Ah, you're a greedy dog," I laughed, delighted at his about-turn. "You always want another treat and it's hardly surprising, with everything you've been through."

Still, I was starting to panic. Just as I wondered if I'd have to pick him up and carry him back to the kennels, Bailey took a cautious step forward, and then another. I breathed again. "Let's go this way; let's avoid those sheep and head down to the furthermost field, where you can have some time off the leash."

Every couple of paces, Bailey stopped and looked around again. Perhaps he had felt safer the first time we came out because Christine was there as well. Perhaps having two of us with him had made him feel more secure.

By now, I was willing him to rediscover his courage, to keep going. It suddenly felt important to make him complete this walk, like it would be a huge setback for him to give up.

Over the years I'd trained hundreds of dogs, and often at moments like this, it was pure gut instinct that told me what to do. My instinct now was to keep going, to break through his hesitancy and show him how the world would feel with no leash, no metal chain, no racing track to contain him. I realized now that I wanted desperately for him to feel free, perhaps for the first time in his life.

"Okay, Bailey, now we're going to move one step, that's it. And another. Good boy."

I carried on reassuring him, talking to him like a newborn baby. As we continued on, painfully slowly, a goose appeared in the adjoining paddock, honking at the horses who munched on grass without a glance in its direction. Bailey stiffened. I could tell he was about to bolt. His ears quivered. He stepped backward. His eyes seemed to swivel in his head.

"Bailey, it's all okay, it's nothing to worry about. That's just another silly goose wanting our attention. Just stay with me, stay here with me," I crooned.

The greyhound's ears twitched. He seemed to be in two minds about what to do. The racing animal in him was trembling at the gate, waiting for the sign to pounce, while the rescue animal, the stricken creature who had arrived here, was unsure, sensing perhaps that the time for chasing on command was over.

"Steady there, darling, steady. He'll do no harm to you."

For a moment we both stood there, suspended in time. Luckily, the moment passed, and Bailey put his head down again and resumed his slow trot behind me. Really, he was coping so well with all these new experiences. I managed to lead him out of the field and into the area in which we could release him from his leash.

"Well done, boy, what a brave boy you are," I said, showering him with praise. As I stroked him, I reached down and unhooked the leash. "See, Bailey, you're free now. Why don't you go and explore . . ."

I knew that taking him off the leash was risky. As an ex-racer, his predator instincts would have been honed to perfection, and he could easily spy a small animal and bolt off after it. If Bailey was at peak physical health, I don't think I would have risked it. Greyhounds can run at forty miles per hour once they spy their prey. As he was still recovering, I knew the chances of him running for any sustained period of time were low, and he seemed so attached to me, walking right by my side, barely looking too far ahead, I could feel fairly confident that he'd come back to me if I needed to call him. The reason I'd chosen this field was that the fencing all the way around was sturdy, and so he couldn't go far, but even so, I felt a little tense as I watched him. When Bailey realized he was free, he seemed confused. He sniffed around the grass at my feet, gradually getting farther and farther away from me, but he didn't race off, at least not yet.

"You and me have a lot in common, boy," I mused as I sat on a tree stump. I was feeling shattered. The walk had really been too much for me as well, but, like Bailey, I knew I had to push myself a little each day in order to break the cycle of illness and weakness.

"I know what it is to feel neglected, even though you have suffered torments I can only guess at. As a child, I clung to

my dad because he was the only one who showed me any affection. My mother always seemed to dislike me, and I never
found out why until quite recently."

Bailey looked up at me, and I took that to be a sign to
carry on.

"I hurt very deeply. From a very young age, I knew my
mother didn't love me. She made it very clear she preferred
my brother and my younger sister Pam, who was ten years
younger than me. She would always say: 'You are such a mess,
Barby, that I had to have another girl to make up for it. Pam
can dance but you're completely flat-footed.' Silly things, but
they cut like daggers.

"It was Mum who put down my first-ever pet dog, a mongrel called Rex, while I was at school. I will never forget skip-
ping home to find the house empty. There was no clatter of
paws as Rex came to greet me, no nose pinned to the window
watching for my return. He'd been ill and hadn't been himself,
but even so. . . . I don't suppose I ever forgave her for that
cruelty.

"I don't ever remember Mum holding me, like the other
mothers did when they cuddled their children, but I always
wanted her to. Even as a young woman, I tried to get close
to her. Many years ago, when she was ill in the hospital, I
drove over, picked my brother Peter up, and spent hours at
her bedside in Eastbourne Hospital helping her eat and drink.
I decorated her small front room with a big 'Get Well' sign
on her return. Later, when an aunt visited from Canada, Mum
asked me to come and visit too. Well, something urgent came
up at the sanctuary and I couldn't.

"When I rang the next day, Mum picked up and refused to speak to me, saying, 'I don't have a daughter called Barbara.'" I swallowed down my feelings, gulping in the cold air to calm myself. I didn't often talk about my childhood, and then only really to my animals because they could keep my secrets.

I looked up to see Bailey had moved toward the center of the field, though he hadn't yet tried to run.

"Only my mum ever called me Barbara, everyone else called me Barby. Bailey, you know the depth of human frailties and callousness, you will understand how I felt when my mother finally told me why she'd never loved me as she should, or at least that was my interpretation of it." I paused. A wave of sadness threatened to engulf me. Somehow Bailey's plight had brought up so much of my suffering from the past, leading me to wonder if we ever truly get over the traumas and pain of past injuries and hurts. Grief hit me as I sat there, gazing over the barren, cold fields, the lines of trees reaching their gnarled fingertips to the sky, the occasional throaty cry of a crow settling on the power line that ran across this field. Perhaps this was my crisis point too? Bailey had touched a nerve buried deep within me, showing me that I understood what it is to feel alone and unloved. I grew up wanting my mother's love. Although I acted up as a child, pretending I didn't need her, scowling every time I saw her, I was really doing all that to hide a multitude of emotional wounds. Bailey had suffered the same fate—and I realized that the bond between us, animal and human, had deepened. It was a bond of suffering, and it was the reason I felt so intensely drawn toward this lovely creature. I believe that in looking after a sick, injured, or distressed animal we are in turn healed. There is a kind of magic to caring for our fellow creatures, one that works in mysterious ways that, over the years, had left me in awe of the natural connection between people and pets.

I carried on, speaking out loud although only the birds, trees, blades of grass, the wind, and the dog could hear me.

"There was a tense phone conversation between Mum and myself, oh years ago now. She told me that I was in fact a twin. I'd been born first, and then a second daughter, Patricia, followed after me. Well, Patricia didn't survive the night, and even though Mum never said explicitly that she blamed me for my twin's death, somehow I think she did, and it was the reason why she could never bring herself to care for me. I may be wrong, but it feels like that was what happened. She closed down in her grief at losing a child, and I became a representation of everything she'd lost.

"The human heart is a complex and strange thing, Bailey. We humans make mistakes all the time, as you well know. Mum's first child had been a stillborn daughter, so Peter was in fact the second child to be born to her and Dad but the first to survive. Then she lost Patricia.

"Mum must have suffered too," I told the dog, who had just finished relieving himself against the hedge, making me smile.

"I can't imagine how painful it must be to carry two children and neither of them to survive past the birth. Poor woman. Yes, my mother suffered too.

"My decision not to have children looks pretty sensible in light of all that," I laughed.

I'd had an elective hysterectomy when I was forty. I hadn't wanted the bother of using contraception, and I'd always suffered hugely with my periods as a young woman, so I was quite happy to see the back of my womb, and had never had any regrets. As anyone would tell you, my animals were my children, and there was never any space for a human child to come into my life.

Just then I caught a streak of gray in the corner of my eye. I'd been staring at the sky, which had clouded over to a murky gray, threatening rain. Again, another streak of movement. It couldn't be . . . could it?

Gasping, I looked down to see Bailey running. He was running for joy and the sheer love of it, rather than as a racing dog on a track. I stood up, clapping delightedly as I did so, my tiredness and sadness forgotten in the light of this triumph I was now witnessing. He was agile, fleet-footed. I could see his muscles straining as he ran and ran. He leaped over another stump, he turned quickly on his tail, then swooped back to me once he saw me leaping with joy, all thoughts of suffering dispelled in this glorious moment.

He was worn out as he flopped down at my feet, panting as if he'd run one of his track races.

"You clever, clever dog," I squealed, as tears streamed down my face.

"Look what you've made me do, I'm blubbing like a baby!" I laughed, bursting with happiness. Bailey had come through the worst and out the other side—I could sense it as if we truly were connected in spirit as well as circumstance. His joy at running through a field filled me with hope for the future. The past was the past, that's where it should stay, I saw that now.

"Come on, Bailey, come and give me a cuddle," I said, opening my arms to him and laughing as he stepped up into them, licking my cheek as he did so. Bailey was showing me that we could all start again, that things really could change, and it was never, ever too late. I felt giddy, even though the weather had set in and it was drizzling again.

"Why don't we set off home and tell everyone what a clever boy you are? We can come back another day.

"You're becoming yourself again, Bailey, and perhaps that's what I must do too," I pondered as we started back toward the kennels, me with my hood up and Bailey trotting peacefully now on the leash beside me.

Chapter 13

KINDRED SPIRITS

"Here they are. I can see the car pulling into the driveway," I said to Di, peering at the line of CCTV images that showed me what was going on at several points on the site. It was the morning of my last radiation therapy session, and my friends Elaine and Rob were here to take me to Brighton Hospital.

The day had dawned bright, but there was still a chill wind. I made sure to wear extra layers, as the treatment always left me more vulnerable to the cold.

A few minutes later, Elaine poked her head around the living room door.

"Ready, are we, madam?" She liked to make fun of our situation by making out that I was a grand duchess being looked after by maidservants.

I chuckled my response, and, attempting my most ridiculous posh accent, I said, "Yes, my dear, I am ready. Now take me to the car, will you, please?"

"She really is becoming a lady of the manor," grinned Rob. "Come on, m'lady, I'll carry your bag to the car."

"Are you ready?" Elaine asked kindly.

I smiled at her in response. "It's my last session. It's been a blimmin' nuisance going to the hospital most days, and I'm so glad it's almost over," I said sincerely. "This day couldn't have come soon enough for me, and I'm guessing you both feel the same.

"Who's looking after Bailey today?" I turned to Diane, suddenly panicked.

She shrugged in response. "I think it's Christine, but today that's the least of your worries. Bailey will have someone with him, so let us worry about him while you go and do what you need to do."

Diane could be firm with me. She was quite right, though. It was a big day today, and all I should have been concentrating on was getting through it, one last time.

Elaine's blonde bob disappeared out of the front door, with Rob carrying my bag. I liked to bring a snack, a book, and an extra sweater with me every time I went to the hospital. I looked around at my familiar surroundings: the sunroom was lit up by daylight, my armchair was covered in cushions and rugs, and my trophy cabinet was filled to the brim with cups and medals.

"Come on then, m'lady, it's time to go. Where is she?" I heard Elaine's voice calling from outside.

I took one last look around my home, the place where I felt safe and happy, and turned on my heels. Gabby was standing behind me, her tail wagging, making little high-pitched sounds. I knelt down to kiss her, and she covered my face in licks.

"Stop it, that's enough, you naughty girl," I said affectionately. I could never really tell off my beloved pets.

"I'm coming, I'm just saying goodbye to Gabby," I shouted back, before handing Gabby to Diane, who was hovering in the kitchen.

"Take good care of her, and make sure Fran is with Bailey all day. I want to hear about it if he's not," I told her firmly. I knew I was being overcautious, but a part of me couldn't quite believe that this was really the last time I'd be heading to the hospital for treatment.

"Off you go. You're not going away forever, Barby, you'll be back before 3 p.m. and can spend as much time as you like with that gorgeous greyhound once you're feeling better," laughed Diane, shooing me out of the door.

With that, I made my way out through the gate, making sure it clicked shut as I pulled it to. Elaine and Rob were already in the car.

"I was just about to beep for you," grinned Rob, as I clambered into the back seat.

Just as we started to pull out of the driveway, I saw Bailey coming out into the grassed section of the kennel run, an area with the high chicken wire-style fencing to keep the dogs— and sometimes possibly humans—safe. The greyhound was sniffing the ground and moving in a zigzag fashion, navigating the area that, by now, he knew so well. He was still painfully thin, but there was an eagerness to explore, a new spirit about him that we had nurtured and grown over the past weeks, and in that moment I saw it clearly as if for the first time. The sun was shining though it was a cold day; Bailey looked lean, and there was a soft sheen on his fur which hadn't been there before. He was looking more and more like a healthy dog, albeit one who still needed feeding up.

As the car moved, he looked up and his eyes met mine. I could clearly see them sparkle, a life in them that simply hadn't been there when he had arrived.

Once at the hospital, we trooped through the familiar corridors to the oncology department where the radiotherapy took place. I was handed a robe by a smiling nurse and told to get changed.

"They're ready for you now, Miss Keel. This is your last session, so that's good news, isn't it?" she beamed.

I took the flimsy fabric, which I'd always hated wearing. My bum always hung out of it, and it felt very undignified indeed. Today I didn't mind, though. It was the last time, and I couldn't have been more relieved and happy.

As usual, it took longer to undress than the actual treatment lasted in its entirety. I lay down. The machine did its thing, then I was told I could go. It was as easy as that.

As I pulled off that damned robe, and put my trousers and fleece back on, feeling like a prisoner suddenly set free from jail, the reality that these treatments were over truly hit me. Emotions welled up inside me. My eyes filled with tears, making the room blur. It was over. It was finally done, and now I could rest and recover, hopefully free from cancer and free from the fear of it returning. The tears started to run, and I wiped them away quickly in case someone saw me crying. I don't know why I was feeling self-conscious. That ward must've seen many a tear shed over the years.

I knew the next few days wouldn't be easy as I would experience the same side effects of soreness, fatigue, and nausea. But I also knew that once I'd got past those, I would start to feel more like my old self again.

Stepping out of the cubicle, I was pleased to see Elaine and Rob waiting for me. I think they had realized I was "having a moment," as my dad used to say, and had held back, giving me the space and privacy I needed.

"Oh, you remembered me this time, did you?" I joked as I stepped out, referring to a time once when they'd walked off with my clothes and gone for a coffee, leaving me shivering and semi-naked in my drafty robe. How I'd told them off on their return!

"Well, we nearly forgot and went home. How would you have liked that, you feisty old bird?" Elaine teased, quick as anything.

Her eyes, sharp as a bird's, took in my tear-streaked face. She looked at me fondly, and, just as quickly, we both smiled at each other, then we started to giggle, then burst into peals of laughter. I don't think either of us knew why we suddenly found the situation hilarious. After weeks of tension, perhaps it was just a mighty release. In any case, life felt good again in that moment of hilarity. My friends were here supporting me. My sanctuary was being looked after. I had finished radiation therapy and could start recovering and living my life again, and Bailey was on the mend. I just needed to get through the next few days and there would be light at the end of the tunnel.

Once the journey home was underway, the familiar burning pain returned, beating against my left side like a drum. The exhaustion seemed to come from nowhere. I sank my head back on the headrest and just watched the world flash by as Rob drove us all back to Bexhill.

I felt a wave of gratitude for my friends' help. I knew I could never repay them, and I also knew they would never expect me to. I was a lucky woman, despite everything.

Rob pulled the car into the driveway off Freezeland Lane, and I looked up eagerly to see if Bailey was still there. He wasn't. The weather had shifted from sunlight to gray cloud and I felt my spirits sink a little, though I knew that was the effect of the cancer treatment, which was hitting me with full force now. My earlier optimism and lightness of spirit had been replaced by a low feeling, a tiredness that seeped into my bones, to the depth of my being. Still, I felt disappointed that Bailey hadn't been there to see me on my return.

Once inside I dragged my body onto my bed, and, fully clothed, I lay down, noting the fresh crop of hairs that appeared on my pillow each day. I had been told categorically that it was with chemo that people lost their hair and not radiation therapy, but by now I'd realized that, for me, this wasn't true. I was losing my hair, and, no matter what the consultant had said, it was falling out more and more as each day passed. When I pulled it back into a ponytail there was hardly any thickness to it at all. I hadn't faced up to it because so much else was going on, but now I knew I had to.

As a young woman I'd been attractive, and my hair, which I styled on the order of Dusty Springfield's beehive, had been thick and blonde. But since I'd found my vocation of looking after animals, I'd been less and less concerned about my appearance. After all, it was completely irrelevant when it came to cleaning out the sheep shed! However, the visible loss of my locks had started to disturb me. When Bailey first came to us, he had patches of fur missing. There was something sad about the way that looked because it reflected his ill health and the terrible treatment of him. I felt the same way about my hair coming out. To prove my point, I reached up and grabbed a handful of my once-lustrous locks and, pulling away, I felt the hair come out of my scalp. Barely a tug and it was loose. Bailey's fur was starting to grow back, but I doubted I'd be so lucky.

Where had my life gone? Where was that young woman who wowed the sailors in her bikini? All I could do was accept that the aging process—and this damned cancer—had robbed me of the last vestiges of my youth.

A memory came flooding into my mind. I was a child aged six and I'd been treated for ringworm. In those days, it was usual to shave the child's head, and that's what happened. My mother took me to Brighton Hospital and I was shaved until I was bald. Mum made me wear a hat afterward to reduce my embarrassment, or perhaps hers, at having the condition. Every night she'd peer at my head, berating me because there was no sign of new hair growth. This went on for six months then, one day, I was sitting doing a puzzle by the window. It was a sunny day, a bit like today, at the start of spring, and all of a sudden she shrieked, making me jump out of my skin.

"Barbara, your hair's growing. Look, I can see it. At last, you've got fuzz on your head."

She walked me to a mirror so I could see for myself, and there it was, the first new growth of hair appearing on my scalp. How strange to remember that right now, after years of forgetting it ever happened. In my mind's eye I could vividly see the delight on my face as I stroked the top of my head and felt the shadow of hair returning. My happiness was partly due to the fact that I'd spent the last few months being bullied at school for having no hair. Some of the kids made fun of me relentlessly, and I wondered if that experience, in part, had made me into the feisty, take-no-nonsense character that I am today.

I certainly learned to defend myself, which was not such a bad thing. Still, the memories were painful, and I had to re-mind myself that those days were long gone, and no one at the shelter cared about whether I had hair or not now. The fact that I was the boss also meant that if anyone did try to tease me about my hair loss, they'd be out on their ear.

"It doesn't matter," I said aloud, making both Gabby and Harry poke their heads up and look at me. I laughed at their quizzical expressions.

"Neither of you care whether I've got hair or not, do you, dearies?" I said, ruffling Gabby's fur first, then turning to pat Harry. "And neither does Bailey. He's got more courage in his front paw than most humans have in their whole body. I'm going to follow his example and not care a jot that my hair is shedding. Perhaps I'll like being bald."

I was making a joke of it, as it was the only way to look at life. You either laughed or you cried, and today I chose laughter.

"Let's find out what is going on with that greyhound, shall we?" I carried on speaking aloud just for the hell of it. Picking up the walkie-talkie that was always at my side, I buzzed Christine.

"Hello, dear, can you hear me?"

"Loud and clear, Barby. How can I help you?" Christine replied right away.

"I'm all right, dear, but a little tired, and I really want to know how Bailey is getting on today. Today's session has left me absolutely shattered, and I just don't have the energy to walk over. Would you mind very much if you came over and filled me in?" I asked.

Gabby cocked her head to one side. She really did look like the most adorable dog. I held her little face close to mine and let her give me doggie kisses on my cheeks and chin.

"No problem, Barby, I'll be there in a jiffy," Christine said. Ten minutes later and there was a knock on my bedroom door.

"Come in, dearest," I called from the bed. Christine opened the door and came in. She sat on the chair next to me.

"You're in the right place, though you look very pale. Can I get you anything?" she asked, her face a picture of concern. Christine was always sensitive to other people's problems and was extremely empathetic.

"I'm fine, really I am. I just need to rest up, it's been quite a journey," I sighed. Christine couldn't help but agree.

"Well, you don't do yourself any favors. All those cold mornings sitting out with Bailey, it's no wonder you're ailing," she frowned.

"Now don't go fussing over me. I wanted to be with the greyhound, it was important. And that's what I wanted to ask you about. I just wanted to check he's had a good day," I said, resting my head back on my pillows.

"Well, he's doing really well. All of a sudden he seems to be improving rapidly. Obviously he's still underweight even for a greyhound but I think we should start to think about rehoming him," she answered, taking me completely by surprise.

Of course I knew we would find a home for him eventually, but I honestly hadn't thought it would be so soon. I felt shocked at the truth of it. It was essential that Bailey found a loving, permanent new home; it was just that the thought of seeing him go felt extremely upsetting.

"Oh," was all I could say in response.

Christine leaned forward and patted my hand.

"I know it's early days, but he really is doing very well. He has a lovely temperament, which is normally the main issue with dogs that have been abused. As you know, they can become unpredictable and are harder to rehome once they become stronger and start acting aggressively. That isn't the case with Bailey. He has the sweetest, gentlest character of any dog I know."

Christine paused. She was watching me, and my expression must've given away how suddenly distraught I felt. I didn't want Bailey to go, and I have never been able to hide my feelings.

"He is eating well now," Christine continued. "He wants treats all the time. He's keeping down four small meals a day, and the medication has worked brilliantly. His sores are almost gone, though he still has dry skin and sore feet, but in time those things will resolve too. We have to say goodbye to him one day; I just think it would be worth looking for someone to take him on before we become any more attached."

Christine spoke kindly. She was looking into my eyes as she spoke. I knew by saying "we" she really meant me. She was right, though. I'd fallen for that brave little soul in the kennels, but I also knew that he deserved a lovely new home with people who could devote their lives and time to him, which was something I couldn't do with everything I had to deal with at the sanctuary.

I saw the sense of what she was saying and silently nodded my head in response.

"Good, that's good, Barby. Perhaps we can put out some feelers? There will be plenty of people who'd love to take on such a lovely dog. He's a real sweetie."

Over the weeks, I had watched Bailey slowly recover. I'd witnessed his natural bravery and his unquenched instinct for love. He'd taught me so much in the two months we'd had the privilege of caring for him. Seeing his injuries—and his courage in facing new challenges and letting people get close to him—had helped me overcome so many of my own demons. He only wanted to be loved. It was a remarkable achievement after everything he'd been through.

It was my turn to help him by looking for the best possible new home for him. I knew I would be devastated when he left, but I also knew I had grown stronger as a result of caring for him. The thought of losing this special dog was heartbreaking, but I owed him so much, and I vowed then and there to do everything in my power to create a wonderful new life for him, free of his past, a whole new future full of the love he deserved so very much.

Chapter 14

NEW BEGINNING

"Oi, dozeychops, it's your turn to make tea," I shouted out to Fran, who was clattering cups in the kitchen sink.

"I'm already making you one, you old bat," he called back. I grinned. Fran always gave as good as he got, even though he currently had his own problems. I had just found out that I wasn't the only one with cancer: Fran had been diagnosed with skin cancer. A life spent outside looking after animals had left him with the illness, and yet nothing in his manner had changed at all. He still bantered with me and the rest of the staff and carried on with his duties in exactly the same way as he had before. I respected the way he shrugged off his diagnosis, even laughing about it, saying it was ironic because he'd been vegan since a young lad and therefore thought himself safe from the dreaded C-word.

"Thank you, dear," I said in a much sweeter tone of voice when he walked in and handed me my hot tea.

"I'm not going to be here for the rest of the week as I have to go to the hospital and have tests to see if it has spread," he said, as nonchalantly as if he was telling me about the weather.

"Okay, dearest. If there's anything you need, any help at all, you will let me know, won't you?" I said, unable to keep the concern from my voice.

Fran understood, but he replied, "I refuse to die of cancer. I've got too much to do. All I want is a diagnosis, and then I'll deal with it my own way."

I nodded. There was no point getting dramatic about it. Lots of ordinary people dealt with cancer every day, and it wasn't splashed on a newspaper front page. We simply had to face up to it and do the best we could to keep living.

I instantly thought of Bailey and his indomitable spirit, and how he had found a new lease on life with us. As my health improved daily, so did his, and as well as his physical recovery, he was blossoming as an affectionate, obedient, loving dog. Every time I saw him, he was more confident. He seemed less startled by sudden noises, like a door slamming shut in the breeze or the roar of the tractor engine starting nearby. Now he was showing real curiosity about the world, especially as spring had arrived and we were able to have many more walks around the site. He loved his walks, though I hadn't been brave enough to take him off the leash again. As his strength improved, I thought it more likely that he might bolt away after a field creature, and so he stayed on a long leash, clearly more and more happy and carefree each time. He reveled in the sights and sounds around the sanctuary, and had become much more confident when faced with the wild horses or the crowing cockerels. They had become the backdrop to his life, and even though we'd discussed rehoming him, I think a part of me hoped he would stay here with us, enjoying the feel of grass under his paws and the scents of all the small creatures that lived here on the site.

Today I had said to Christine that I would accompany her and Bailey on their usual morning walk. The spring sunshine that greeted me when I awoke had lifted my mood and reminded me that I had come through darkness and survived. Now it was time to start *thriving* again, and the first thing I wanted to do was to join the greyhound and my beloved friend on a walk that would span the heart of the sanctuary land. I couldn't think of a more perfect way to start the day—and remind myself of all the beauty that surrounded me and my motley crew here in the Sussex landscape.

Walking over to the kennels, Dan stopped with his wheelbarrow filled with hay bales.

"Barby, just to let you know, I'm getting the vet out for Little Booja," he said, stopping me in my tracks.

"Oh dear, what's the matter with the goat now?" I asked. Little Booja had ongoing problems with his front legs, and we couldn't figure out what was wrong.

"He's struggling to move in the heat," said Dan. "One of his back legs now seems sore. The vet gave him steroids last time he was here, but we need to check him out again, maybe get some tests done," Dan replied, pushing his glasses back up his nose. He was sweating due to his exertion and the fact it was an unseasonably warm day.

"Yes, you must get the vet out, no problem," I said. "Hang the expense, I can't abide seeing an animal in pain."

Dan grinned his reply and made off, trundling the hay up to the farm animals' enclosures.

Our vet bills ran to £4,000 a month on average, and the sanctuary itself needed £6,000 a month just to keep going. It was no wonder I spent so much of my time calling local businesses, begging for their help or sponsorship. Our annual bazaars in the summer and at Christmas brought in about £16,000 between them, but this was really only enough to cover us for just under three months. It was an expensive business running an animal sanctuary, and we received no public funding. Everything we raised was through our own efforts. The shop in Bexhill was an important and consistent source of funds, as were our loyal supporters who donated each month or left us money in their wills. We relied upon these generous donations to keep our open-door policy and our vow that no animal would be destroyed unless it was cruel to keep it alive. This meant we were always fit to bursting with abandoned creatures.

I thought about the gargantuan task that faced us each month and how each month we seemed to scrape by somehow.

"Barby, you look preoccupied," Christine said as I met her and Bailey outside the kennel building.

"Oh it's nothing, dear. I'm not going to let anything worry me today. How's my gorgeous boy?" I bent down to greet Bailey, whose tail was wagging, grateful to rest my thoughts about money and upkeep. Vet bills were a fact of our life here, and there was no way I'd let an animal suffer, so I had to accept there was a cost to that, which I gladly paid.

Bailey felt solid to my touch, like he was finally back to where he always should have been with his weight and muscle tone. I patted his flank, taking the opportunity to run my hand down his spine and feel for his rib cage, and was gratified to feel the flesh that now coated him.

"That prescription diet has worked a treat. He was so lucky not to have real lasting damage from his mistreatment. He seems to have responded well to all of the medical and dietary intervention, which is always a good sign," Christine said as I stroked him.

Nodding, I said: "Let's give us both a run, shall we?" Bailey was such an elegant, dignified dog. His long legs started to trot, and I felt that warm familiarity between dog owner and pet, the connection that exists when both move forward in harmony. As we set off, heading down into the lane as we trekked around the boundary of my land, I felt my heart soar. Everyone deserved a new beginning. We had given Bailey his, and now it was my turn to take a leaf out of his book.

I was still slow in comparison to Christine and the dog, who had come on in leaps and bounds, but I was improving every day, and could now walk for up to two hours—a huge improvement.

I looked down at Bailey's legs as we walked and was pleased to see the sores had all but vanished.

"Here, boy, look what I've got for you," I said, taking a

treat from my pocket. Bailey quickly took it from my outstretched hand.

"Always hungry, aren't you, boy?" I said. It still made me
sad to see how eagerly he responded to any suggestion of food.
Perhaps he would always carry the memory of being starved,
the anxiety of where the next meal would come from. It was
a terrible legacy to leave a dog.

Christine and I fell into a steady rhythm, one where we
had no need of words as we walked. I began to hum to myself,
and the sound of Bailey's paws in contact with the earth as
we moved was music to my ears. I held my face up to the
sunshine, feeling the warmth saturate my skin. It was such
a welcome reprieve from winter, and I felt a fresh surge of
happiness. The future was unknown but it held all the possibility of the flowers about to bud. The past was over, Bailey
had shown me that, and all that we ever had was the present.
Today, as the green fields stretched out around us, the
hedgerows bursting with vibrant life, I knew I was one of
the lucky ones. I breathed in the smell of the grass and soil,
knowing this was where I belonged, feeling it in every cell
of my body.

Later that day, the residents of a local rehabilitation center
were due in to help look after the animals. I liked the thought
of giving anyone, whatever they'd done, whoever they'd been
beforehand, a second chance to make a positive difference.
Several local groups, including those that helped people with
special needs, and now this rehab unit for former drug addicts,
were involved with the Barby Keel Animal Sanctuary, and I
encouraged anyone with a love for feathered or furry friends

to come and be a part of what we were doing. I believe that work like this, giving back to the community in some way, helps rebuild self-worth and confidence. I'd seen people with distressing emotional and mental health issues walk through our gates and, over time, rediscover their innate sense of themselves. I'd seen people blossom as they learned about the animals and how best to care for them, a feeling that gave them a new identity and sense of self.

Animals did that to you, if you were open to their healing powers. In the very act of taking care of them, many people found themselves transformed, their social skills improving and their ability to engage with life enhanced. Obviously there were those who resisted these changes, or who were simply too mentally unwell to respond, but those cases were few and far between.

At 2 p.m. on the dot, the gate opened, and a small group of five men arrived. They were dressed in jogging tops and bottoms, some of them dragging on hand-rolled cigarettes as they sauntered into the sanctuary.

Dan appeared from the workshop and led them out toward the farm animals. I watched them go, the men joshing with each other, Dan turning round to join in the banter. I knew each and every one of those men would work damn hard that day. They had the unenviable task of cleaning out the pigs and horses, replacing the soiled straw with fresh bedding, and it was good to see how they all rose to the task and got on with it. Some of the men stopped in for a cup of tea at the same time as the rest of the volunteers, and it was heartening to see how polite and hardworking they were.

We all have problems in life, and I believe strongly that we should never judge anyone too harshly. There is always a reason why people behave the way they do. I would even say that about Bailey's previous owners now. At first I'd wanted to kill them when I saw the state of the pitiful creature, but now I just felt pity for them to have been so unhappy, so unloved themselves that they could do that to another living creature. I don't know why I'd mellowed in my attitude toward them. Perhaps it was because in the end they did the right thing in dumping Bailey here, and we were able to save him and bring him back to his old self. Or perhaps it was simply that I'd been through so much during Bailey's stay here, and those experiences had left their mark, made me more likely to forgive, though never, ever forget. Perhaps I had let go of some of my childhood hurts in nurturing the greyhound back to health, which in turn made me less quick to defend or attack. I didn't know why, but something had definitely shifted.

I sipped my afternoon cuppa watching the people, young and not-so-young, drink coffee and tea together, all here for the same reason: to give the love our animals so desperately needed—and the sight of them all made my struggles fade away as the day wound to a close and twilight made its creeping entrance over the land.

Chapter 15

Rehoming

A huge number of people contact us saying they want a new addition to their household. We usually invite them to drop into the sanctuary to meet and greet the animals, either mooching around the cattery with Diane on hand to answer questions, or by visiting the kennels to see which of the residents might appeal.

Sometimes the people leave without making a connection to a dog or cat, but usually they spot one, or even more, that they are drawn to. Once potential new owners have chosen their prospective pet, they are then subject to a series of checks done by Brenda to see that their lifestyle and home life are suitable for the animal they've picked. A home visit will follow, and then, once Brenda is satisfied, the necessary forms are filled out, any instructions regarding medication are given, and then finally the animal is free to go home with them. There is usually a two-week delay in between choosing a new pet and receiving it, which also gives people a "cooling-off" period.

We are very clear about the kinds of families each animal might need. For instance, a cat that may have been mistreated by children would go to a child-free home, a dog that is disturbed by loud noise is perhaps not best suited to living by a busy main road. There is also the innate personality of the animal to consider and the preferences and needs of their breed. An intelligent, sensitive, and gentle dog like Bailey would most likely not be suited to a busy home with children. As greyhounds are built for speed, not endurance, he would not need to be walked for miles every day, though being somewhere with access to a contained area where he could let rip and sprint a couple of times a week would be preferable. As a greyhound's hunting instincts are so finely honed, especially with ex-racers, living with a cat or small dog could be tricky. We hadn't really tested Bailey's "cat compatibility," but I felt safe saying to Christine that we should reject anyone who came from a home with cats.

"He'll just chase them all day and maybe even kill them. We can't risk it," I said, sitting down in my armchair.

Christine had joined me at the bungalow for a chat about who we should look for when rehoming Bailey. I'd been through my big book of names, which contained all the people who had rung in saying they wanted specific animals, without yet yielding any results.

"He's such a sensitive boy. Greyhounds hate being around any tension in a household, so it really does have to be a settled, caring place that he goes to," Christine added.

"I have put out a few feelers. I have some friends who know

some people who might be looking for a greyhound, but I'll let you know when I find out more."

I nodded. Somehow the thought of losing him didn't seem real. I was talking about letting go of Bailey, but I hadn't really yet faced up to the fact that this could become a reality. Bailey had made such an impact on all of us. Everyone at the sanctuary spoke about him constantly, swapping notes about what he'd eaten that day, how many walks he'd had. He was part of our lives, and I knew it would rip my heart out to say goodbye, a thought I tried to bury whenever it emerged. I felt such a confusing mixture of emotions: sorrow at the thought of letting him go, happiness that he'd made such leaps forward, and pride in his ability to learn to trust again through the gentleness and care he had been shown here. I was also worried that Bailey might feel he'd been abandoned again by the very fact of rehoming him, and that thought had been giving me yet more sleepless nights.

Some of my feelings must've shown on my face.

"Barby, he'll only be rehomed to the right people, in a permanent loving home that will only be the best for him," Christine told me kindly. "We will make sure he is comfortable and happy with his new owners before the rehoming takes place. The whole process will be made as easy as possible for him . . ."

". . . and me," I replied, looking up at her. I was embarrassed to realize that my eyes had filled with tears.

"Oh come here, you silly woman," Christine laughed, pulling me up and into a hug. "He has to go, you know that, don't you? He can't stay here. We won't be able to give him one hundred percent attention once he's better and that in itself might make him feel strange. It will be best for him to find people who can carry on what we've done here, by lavishing him with the attention he deserves." She smiled kindly, standing back and inspecting me.

"Are you sure you're okay, Barby?"

"Of course I am, I just can't keep my eyes from leaking," I grumbled, rubbing away the tears.

The hunt for a suitable rehoming couple or person had officially begun. Two days later, Christine knocked on the door of the living room where I was scrutinizing paperwork for an upcoming charity trustees meeting. Each quarter I presented the updated accounts and I was going over the bookkeeper's workings before the others arrived.

"It's only me. I have some news," she said, poking her head around the door.

I stopped for a moment, and I'm sure I felt my heart beat faster. I somehow sensed what was to come and dropped the papers onto my lap.

"Don't worry, everything's fine. I just wanted to let you know that I think I've found the right people to take Bailey," she continued, her tone gentle. Christine knew that, however good this news was for the dog, it would still be hard for me to hear.

There was a moment's silence while I digested her words.

"You'd better tell me everything then, dearest," was all I could say. I collected my papers together and placed them on my desk. This needed my full concentration.

Christine sat down beside me and began: "Unbelievably, within hours of our conversation about finding a home for Bailey, my friend rang me to say that she knew of a retired couple looking for a greyhound. They have two already and want another companion dog."

It seemed too good to be true, and I couldn't ignore the sinking feeling of disappointment in my stomach at the thought of Bailey leaving us. The couple sounded perfect, though their suitability would, of course, be subject to our rigorous testing procedures.

Christine continued: "They want to come in and see Bailey. How are you fixed later today? We could take them through to meet him and see if there's a connection. They're local so won't be coming far. Do you need some time to think about it?"

"No, dear," I smiled, "it's all right. They certainly sound like they could be the right fit for him, so yes, please ring them and tell them to come in this afternoon. It's important that they get to meet him and for us to start assessing them as soon as possible." I kept my tone light and upbeat, but inside my heart was breaking. Christine's head bobbed in agreement, and she patted my arm gently before hurrying off to call them, leaving me sitting alone in the living room.

Now get a grip, Barby, I told myself firmly. *This lovely dog needs an equally lovely home to go to. He has to start the next chapter of his life—and it's about time you did the same . . .*

I looked down at the papers on my lap and sighed. It was no use. I hadn't even begun to process my feelings about

Bailey being rehomed, and it all felt like it was happening so fast.

He has to go, you know that, old girl, I continued, *he has to go . . .*

Just then, Dan put his head round the doorway. "We're all here and ready for the trustees meeting. You okay?"

"I'm fine, Dan. Absolutely fine. You just go through, I'll be with you in a minute," I answered, plastering a smile on my face and gathering up the documents for the meeting. I couldn't show my feelings to the people who relied upon me. I had to keep going and hope that my heart would catch up with my head when it came to the matter of our beloved Bailey finding a new home.

Later that day, I was pacing around the kennels, with Bailey watching me in his placid way, still and serene, while I was like a whirling dervish as I waited impatiently for the prospective new owners to arrive. Part of me wanted them to be completely unsuitable: to have screaming children, five cats, and a tiny yard. The other, better, part of me wanted them to be utterly reliable, secure, friendly people with a passion for greyhounds and a yard big enough for him to run free. I knew I was being daft. Most animals that came in to us were eventually rehomed, so it shouldn't have been big news to me, but I had formed a deep attachment to this creature. His struggles had mirrored mine, and even though neither of us was completely recovered yet, we had both come such a long way together. It was unbelievably sad to think that we would now part company—but I had to keep a brave face. This was for the best. I wanted Bailey to go to a loving home; I just wasn't completely ready to say goodbye yet.

The door to the kennels opened and Christine strode in. She was chatting happily to a nice-looking couple.

"This is Mary, and this is Ron, and they've come to see Bailey," she smiled, touching my arm lightly in a small but warm gesture of support.

"Hello, I'm Barby Keel, welcome to my sanctuary," I said, greeting them in my usual way.

"Hello, Barby, it's so lovely to meet you. Oh, and this must be Bailey! Well, isn't he an absolute beauty . . ." Mary exclaimed, spotting the dog standing behind me.

Bailey's streamlined, muscular body looked relaxed in the electric light. His ears were pricked forward as he waited to see who these new people were, but he remained calm and settled.

I looked down at him as if for the first time, and in his proud bearing I saw the lineage that went back thousands of years. He was still some way from peak fitness, but I could see how graceful, how athletic his build was, how he and his breed could run faster than a horse at top speed. His eyes were intelligent and curious, watching everything, while his manner was affectionate and gentle to the point of tenderness. I felt a swell of feeling for him. These people were sure to fall in love with him just as I had done.

Mary had walked straight over to him and was feeding him a treat, while stroking his sides. Ron was looking at them both. They seemed spellbound.

I looked over at Christine who was smiling back at me, and I nodded. It seemed that we had indeed found the right owners.

"Of course you'll need to spend some time with him here and introduce your two other greyhounds to him before we can look at rehoming, and we'll need to do a site visit to check your home. Christine will take charge of all that," I said conversationally, but I don't think they heard me. Both of them were utterly taken by the dog and were now kneeling next to him, fussing over him, and telling him what a gorgeous boy he was.

"Have you rehomed before? Were your other dogs from shelters?" I asked, keen to find out as much as I could about their situation.

"Yes," replied Ron, "both our other two were from rescue shelters—and they settled with us straightaway. We've never had any problems with them."

"Bailey will need to meet you both a few times so we know if he'll fit in with the others or not," I explained, though I didn't have too many concerns about that. Greyhounds were originally bred to hunt in packs, so their aggression toward other dogs had been almost completely wiped out.

"He's an absolute poppet," Mary sighed, getting back up to her feet and beaming at me. "What do we need to do now?"

At this point Christine took over. Bailey had been her charge for his stay, and so she would be the one who oversaw the next steps.

"Christine will talk you through it. We'll set up a few times for you to visit Bailey with your dogs and we'll go for walks to make sure everyone's happy. It was nice to meet you, and hopefully I'll see you again soon," I smiled at them as I left, swallowing a lump that had formed in my throat.

There was always the chance that they might change their minds and not go ahead with taking on Bailey, but somehow I doubted it. I saw the looks in their eyes—it had been love at first sight.

Chapter 16

ALL CLEAR

"I'm delighted to tell you that your cancer does not appear to have spread, and we can officially give you the all clear." Dr. Allen leaned over his desk and thrust his hand forward. I shook it, my own trembling, as my body fought to catch up with my mind. The all clear?

"Doctor, does that mean I'm cured?" I asked, my voice sounding incredulous.

"As far as we can tell, yes, it does. Though I still advise you to start taking the tamoxifen tablets, as this can prevent any future problems," he said, taking off his glasses and looking at me a little wearily.

"Dr. Allen, you know my feelings about taking yet more tablets. I won't do it. I'm very grateful for everything you've done for me, but when I make up my mind I don't tend to change it—ever," I told him firmly.

I had to give the man credit. He'd been trying to get me to take those blasted tablets for six years now, but I still resisted. This time I think he realized his words and effort were futile.

"You really are the most exasperating patient, but I'm thrilled for you, Miss Keel, and sincerely hope I never see you again."

I laughed at that.

"And I sincerely hope never to see you again, either, Doctor," I joked back, but meaning every word. I'd been through cancer and I'd come out the other side, but I wouldn't wish it on my worst enemy. I would die happy knowing I'd never see the inside of the oncology department ever again.

When the consultant uttered those wonderful words, Elaine had also breathed out a great sigh of relief. I hadn't really realized until that point how much my friends had suffered watching me go through that hell. It was my turn to squeeze my dear friend's hand, and I did so, feeling my eyes prick with tears. I knew I was one of the lucky ones. So many people are given the same terrible news I was all those months ago and don't survive. I was extremely grateful—but also determined to get back to my previous state of health. I was fighting at the bit to get back out on the land doing the things I loved around the site.

"And don't you think for a minute that you're going to be lifting any heavy sacks of animal food or digging trenches anymore," Elaine turned to me, reading my mind like she always did.

"You still have to take it easy. Tell her, Doctor. She's an absolute shocker. If you tell her she's okay, she'll be out feeding the gulls at the crack of dawn and trying to shift great bales of straw."

Dr. Allen chuckled. "You certainly would be advised not to do any of those things for the present. Enjoy some time off, Barby. Rest and recuperate while you have the chance. You have good friends who take care of you. Just enjoy that rather than taking on too much," he said, smiling.

Rob laughed as soon as he heard those words. "Doctor, you'll never stop Barby Keel from doing too much. It's in her nature, and her sheer bloody-mindedness is probably what has got her through this terrible disease."

I looked round at my friend gratefully, though I knew everything the consultant said was right. I *should* be resting. I *should* enjoy other people looking after me. I *should* be a better patient and wait until I'd recovered completely before taking on any more tasks at the sanctuary, but already my mind was on the never-ending list of things that needed doing. Our Summer Bazaar was two months away, but, even so, there was still much to organize.

"Well, I couldn't do the gulls even if I wanted to, because Diane does them now, so there," I said, poking my tongue out, making Elaine and Rob laugh.

"Don't worry, Dr. Allen," said Elaine, "we'll be on hand to keep an eye on Barby. If she's doing too much, we'll pull her back in line."

I sighed theatrically, though, of course, I loved my friends dearly and couldn't express how grateful I was to them for everything they'd done for me.

I understood that my days hauling bales of hay or lifting

crates of food or sacks of goat mix were probably over, but there was plenty I could do to make myself useful. I could carry on coordinating the volunteers, trustees, and staff. I would continue taking phone calls nonstop throughout the day, and sometimes at night. I would carry on overseeing the cat and dog rehomings, which reminded me: Bailey's prospective new owners were coming out to the site today to go on a walk with us and the dogs. We'd better not hang around much longer if we were going to get back in time.

"Thank you, Doctor. I mean it, though I don't always sound like I do. If there's nothing else I need to know, we'll head back. We have an important rehoming to start today, so we need to get back on the road."

"There's nothing else, except to say well done, Barby. You're in the clear."

We shook hands and I left the consulting room, walking down the corridor and out into the sunshine. It was time to get back to work.

At 4 p.m. that day, Mary and Ron were due to arrive with their two other greyhounds. We'd been back from Brighton for about an hour, so I'd taken the time to have a rest, though I couldn't stop my eyes flicking to the CCTV screen in my living room to check for their arrival. CCTV cameras were positioned discreetly around the site. It was a safety precaution we were forced to take because we had expensive equipment on site, and we'd also run into trouble in the past from a couple of people who'd tried to reclaim their pets long after their cooling-off period had ended—and long after each animal had been successfully rehomed. On both occasions the

previous owners had threatened me personally after I'd explained to them that their pet was no longer theirs. Both had
signed over their rights and responsibilities to the sanctuary,
and neither had contacted us during the seven-day period during which people could change their minds, yet this didn't
keep them from making threats. These days I didn't take any
chances. Dan and his wife were now living on the site in the
trailers closest to the kennels, so I wasn't alone here at nights,
and of course there was Diane, who lived in the annex I built
for my dad years ago.

Nevertheless, I knew Dad hadn't left me completely. There
was a running joke here that he was our resident ghost, as Di
had had some very strange occurrences in her part of the
building.

"Dad's been at it again," she'd say. "Last night I was looking for my cutlery, which turned up in my sock drawer, and
all the pictures on my walls have been turned upside down."

I'd giggle. "He always did have a wicked sense of humor."
Dad really did haunt the annex, playing tricks on Diane, but
none of it scared either of us. His pranks were harmless, and
I felt reassured knowing he was still there somewhere; he
hadn't left me completely when he died.

Suddenly a familiar-looking car pulled into the driveway.
I picked up my walkie-talkie. "Christine, they're here. Would
you mind going to the gate and meeting them, dearest?"

"Right you are, Barby," came her voice in response. Seconds later I saw Christine's figure head out to the gate. She
had Bailey on the leash, and at the sight of them I felt pure
emotion. The dog didn't have a clue what was going on,

though greyhounds are an intelligent breed. We would have to take things slowly so that he got used to these new people. He'd been through so much already, I couldn't bear to think of him feeling upset and confused at having to leave this place.

I pulled on my boots and went out to join them, smiling my welcome as they spotted me.

"Hello, Barby," waved Mary. She was definitely the chattier one of the two.

The couple were both retired, though Mary had mostly been a housewife while Ron worked on the railways, or so Christine had told me. We hadn't yet done the home visit, as Christine wanted to wait and see how Bailey reacted to the other two dogs, which I thought was sensible.

"Hello and welcome to you both. You've met Bailey, so no need for any introductions there. Now, who are these handsome chaps?" I said, bending down to greet the greyhounds.

"This one is called Brandy," Ron said, reaching down to stroke the lighter dog. "She's an old lady, a rescue greyhound; well, they both are. And this one is Flash." Ron patted the head of the darker dog. He was black with almost the same white markings on his face as Bailey, though he had tufts of fur rather than the scant sprinkling Bailey possessed.

Both dogs stood and studied me for a moment before letting me stroke them. Greyhounds had a very regal air about them; in fact, back in the day they were only owned by kings and royalty, and laws were passed to stop commoners from keeping them. I could see their heritage in their long necks and extended graceful bodies.

The three of them together looked impressive. The dogs

sniffed each other, then appeared not to take much more interest in anything other than the treats now being offered to them by Ron. Both Ron and Mary had wide smiles on their faces. They were clearly smitten with our rescue dog, and even as I saw their delighted expressions I couldn't help but feel my heart sink a little. I knew deep down that we had found Bailey's new family, though we would carry out the checking procedures. It is an instinct of mine. I've always been good at seeing through people's motives, and I saw clearly that day how perfect they all were for each other.

"Shall we go for that walk?" I said a little gruffly, emotion starting to get the better of me.

Christine looked over at me, her face mirroring mine. There was a hint of sadness but also great pleasure in seeing the easy relationship between these people and their dogs.

Bailey looked comfortable as Christine took him on the leash, while Ron and Mary each took one of their dogs. We set off, walking down to the end of the drive to the entrance of the sanctuary and turned left down Freezeland Lane. The hedgerows were bursting with life. After the long winter it was such a thrill to see the elderflowers in their white blooms at the roadside surrounded by lush green foliage. I took a deep breath and smelled the honeysuckle that was growing nearby, its scent rising with the heat of the day. There were nettles, chickweed, mallow and even wild garlic, all vying for space in the mass of greenery.

Winters were hard here. We worked outside so much of the year that they felt very long—but when the summer came,

all those months of freezing early morning temperatures, inevitable rainstorms, and blustery winds became a distant memory as the sun warmed our patch of earth and the flowers I
so enjoyed seeing sprang up again, renewed and full of vitality
and life.

As we walked, I felt my own vitality returning. I hadn't
yet regained my previous strength, but I knew then, on that
balmy benign afternoon as the gulls called from the power
lines and the sweet little chiffchaffs trilled their distinctive
high-pitched sound amid the throaty fluting noise of nearby
blackcaps, that everything had turned out just right. I was
free of cancer. Bailey was being given the chance to start his
life again with a new, loving family. Everything was how it
should be.

Every step I took that afternoon was one filled with gratitude. I listened to the others as they chatted about life and
the sanctuary. Christine was marvelous with the couple,
telling them lots of stories about the exploits of some of our
animals, putting everyone at ease. I walked in silence, listening
to the birdsong, smelling the sweet scent of summer grass,
and always, always, glancing over at Bailey, watching his
happy progress as we circled the land, cutting through into
the back fields after half a mile or so. Bailey seemed totally
relaxed trotting alongside Brandy, with Flash walking on the
other side of Mary. The dogs had sniffed each other at first,
their tails wagging, and then they all seemed to settle into a
natural rhythm, walking alongside their humans, enjoying the
smells and sights of the countryside together. In fact, Bailey

looked for all the world like he belonged to this family already, so quickly had they all accepted him.

If Bailey was happy, then I was happy, though I knew my reserve might fail me on the day he left us, but we still had a little more time with him. There was still due process to go through. There were still more walks like this one planned to make sure that Bailey was happy to join this family. There were still days of summer to enjoy together in the perfect harmony that only exists between dog owner and dog, person and pet, human and animal souls coming together to journey through life in companionable happiness. However much I yearned to keep hold of Bailey, it would be unfair to him, and I had two lovable dogs of my own that I needed to spend more time with. Both Harry and Gabby had loved me through my cancer as much as Bailey had, and I loved them both dearly. Their needs had been superseded by Bailey's, but it was time to correct that. It was time for me to let Bailey go, and appreciate what I already had in my life: two daft dogs who slept by me each night, who gave me cuddles and kisses whenever I wanted them, and who were models of contentment and joy.

We started the walk back up toward the sanctuary, and I suddenly felt tired again, my legs shaking a little.

"If you don't mind, dears, I'll stay here for a while and get my breath back," I said.

"Are you okay, Barby? Can I call someone to help you?" Christine looked concerned, instantly fretful about me and my state of health.

"Don't fuss, dearest, I'm just a bit tired today. It's been a long day, and I just want a little bit of peace, if that's okay." I winked at her to show her there really was nothing to worry about.

"All right, if you insist, though if you're not back up at the bungalow in an hour I'll come and find you myself," Christine warned me sternly.

"Goodbye," I called to Mary, Ron, and the dogs as they carried on, walking up through the field toward the main horses' paddock.

It wasn't just tiredness that had made me stop. I wanted to sit down and just soak in the beauty around me. I found a tree stump and sat down on top of it, shutting my eyes for a moment. The birdsong had started for the evening. A plane rumbled overhead. I heard the flapping of wings as birds started to gather farther up the hill on the electricity pylons. Everywhere there was sound: the rustle of small creatures in the grass, the low insistent drone of a nearby bee, the zigzag buzz of a fly. From elsewhere around the sanctuary I heard the chickens clucking and geese honking. The peacocks made their strange unearthly sound, and a random cockerel crowed, getting his voice in early for the evening. A pig grunted, then a dog barked, which set off a chorus of barking.

Everything was as it should be. Animals were being cared for, and my life was coming back into focus. I breathed out the smell of the hospital with its tang of disinfectant. I breathed in the deep lush notes of the trees, bushes, and soil. Life had come full circle. I was back where I belonged, my cancer now a distant memory, or soon to become one. Bailey was looking more and more like a healthy dog with each day that passed, his formerly frail frame filling out nicely. The future was here to greet the both of us.

I smiled a contented smile and sat there, enjoying the moment of tranquillity.

Chapter 17

SAYING GOODBYE

It was the night before Bailey was due to leave. All the re-homing checks had been completed, and Mary and Ron had passed everything with flying colors. Christine had carried out a home visit to ensure Bailey was going to a suitable place. They had a clean, neat home surrounded by a large yard close to stunning countryside. As Ron was retired, they had plenty of time to devote to their dogs, and as both he and Mary were in good health, we were reassured that Bailey would get the exercise he needed. There was plenty of room for Bailey to fit in, and, over the last couple of weeks since that first walk, a bond had developed between him and his new family.

We'd encouraged the couple to visit as much as they could to walk the dogs together. Over the days, Bailey became just as happy trotting on the leash with Ron or Mary, with Christine and me hanging back instead, watching as the dog became more and more used to this new situation.

"He is good as gold," said Christine on one of the last

walks before the rehoming became official. "It's like he just slotted in with them with no fuss, no problems. They really are lucky to have him. Bailey has such a sweet temperament and a gentle manner. All he has ever wanted is someone to love him—well, he has found two lovely people who will do that in spades."

I couldn't have agreed more, and yet the thought of this dog being loved by someone else gave me a pang of grief so sharp I almost stopped walking. For a moment I couldn't speak at all as the emotion swelled within me.

"I'm just so sad to see him go," I said at last. "I can't really believe that he's going at all. I keep thinking that one day I'll wake up and this will all have been a dream and I'll be back in the kennels with him, nursing him and whispering little stories to him as he recovers."

I squinted against the sunshine. I knew Christine would understand. She felt the same way. Looking after Bailey had been a privilege. We had almost certainly saved his life, and with his determination and our continual support, this handsome creature had risen from the ashes to begin a new life, one that meant saying goodbye to the sanctuary and us. Although I still didn't feel ready to see him go, I knew I wouldn't stop him from going.

Bailey was still noticeably skinnier than the other two dogs, but he kept up with them and seemed at peace as he walked with them. I watched as his black figure kept pace alongside Ron, who was holding his leash. The two humans and three dogs paced steadily along the lane, looking for all the world like they'd always been together.

"He's settled with them. I think he'll be happy with Mary and Ron, and that's what's important. And, of course, they adore him too. Well, who wouldn't?" I chuckled, though my heart was both swelling with sheer happiness for how this had all turned out and breaking for the sadness I knew was coming, creeping up all too fast as the days passed and the date for his departure grew nearer.

Summer was well and truly here now, and the initial burst of color from the flowers that grew so abundantly in our part of the world had been replaced by a jungle of plant life around our land. Fran and Dan would be hard at work cutting back hedgerows and pulling up the larger weeds in the animals' enclosures.

"It's a lovely day. Why don't we enjoy it rather than dwell on the negatives? We'll all miss him terribly, but it's time for Bailey to move on," Christine smiled at me kindly.

I could only nod at that.

Back at the sanctuary, the last loose ends regarding the re-homing were tidied up. Bailey's documents were all copied and ready for Mary and Ron to look over and sign. Our vet Stephen had been over to see Bailey, and was amazed at how well the dog had returned to health.

"It's remarkable, truly remarkable. He looks like a different dog. Wonderful work, well done, Barby," he said as he inspected him in the kennel yard.

"Well, it wasn't just me. Christine has worked tirelessly with him, and so has Fran. He's had a lot of support and love from different people here. We're all very sad to see him go," I told him.

"Yes, of course," Stephen replied as he patted Bailey again on the flank and picked up his medical kit, ready to go and see one of the felines who had come in that day: a fairly elderly white cat with black spots on his fur had been handed in by a member of the public after seeing some children torment- ing it. The cat was riddled with tumors, or so Diane believed, and had parts of his ears missing, possibly due to cancer. Di thought the animal was probably in a lot of pain, so we'd called the vet.

Diane was almost in tears as she held and stroked the poor cat. The vet confirmed it was indeed cancer and gave pain re- lief immediately. The prognosis wasn't good, and though we'd only known the cat for a morning, the thought of losing it was upsetting, particularly as it had suffered rough treatment by careless children. It was always hard to fathom how anyone, young or old, could possibly cause an animal pain, but sadly our sanctuary was testament to how prevalent it was, and how much agony some animals endured before they reached our warm, welcoming arms.

Bailey had survived against all the odds, and, even more miraculously, had come out of his own experiences of torment by being *more* loving. He was a remarkable beast, though I'd had to warn Mary and Ron that the rehoming process might unsettle him again.

"He might be confused by his new environment, and may become a little withdrawn and timid again. The sounds, scents, textures and shadows of your home will be completely alien to him. If he's stressed, he'll become a little unresponsive. Greyhounds don't exhibit loud stress behavior, they're more likely to become very quiet and reserved, just as Bailey was when he first came here. All you need to do, as I'm sure you both know, is keep reassuring him kindly and gently. Keep stroking him and be very calm and gentle until he settles in," I explained to the couple as they both sat in my sitting room.

"We understand," said Mary. "We've got him a lovely dog bed to cozy up in and lots of treats to keep him going until he feels at home. Both our other dogs were rescue animals, so we're very aware of what might happen. We know Bailey remains a bit of a challenge given he still needs care, the right food, and his sore feet and dandruff aren't quite right. But rest assured we'll be very tuned in to his needs."

Mary spoke so openly and earnestly I felt reassured that Bailey was indeed going to exactly the right home and the right people. He would finally be given the consistent, long-term love that he had always needed. That was the thought that kept me going as the days passed.

All too soon, it was Bailey's last evening. After all the jobs of the day were finished, and everyone had retired to their part of the site or had gone home, I shut Gabby and Harry inside the bungalow and walked down to the kennels.

As I walked in, Bailey sat up, his tail wagging, before stepping elegantly out of his bed, in the regal way he did, and coming over to me for a cuddle and a kiss.

"Oh yes, you can smell the treat in my pocket, can't you, boy?" I whispered, rustling about in my trouser pocket for the dog biscuits that I knew were Bailey's favorites.

All day I'd felt a churning in my tummy, a knowledge that the hours were ticking past too quickly. I couldn't regret my decision to rehome him. It had been Christine who had set the ball rolling, but it was my ultimate responsibility to approve—or veto—any rehoming. It was the right thing for Bailey. I just needed my heart to recognize that, and I knew it wouldn't be an easy task.

"That's it, you enjoy that. Yes, I have another, you can stop nosing around me, but you'll have to finish that one first."

My voice was filled with affection. I really had grown to love this dog who had been treated so cruelly, and I marveled, as I often did, at what a difference a few months had made. I stroked his coat, which was now soft and had filled out with new fuzzy black fur. I felt his rib cage and haunches, which now lay under a layer of fat and muscle. His nose was wet as he brushed against my hand, nudging me to give him another treat, which of course I did.

Then, out of nowhere, I suddenly burst into tears. I couldn't hold them in any longer. I sobbed like a small child, stroking Bailey and reassuring him as I wept. I couldn't stop. It felt as if a great dam had been broken and I could no longer hold back the torrents of emotion. The endless weeks of cancer treatment and hair loss had taken their toll on me. The ceaseless care and attention we had lavished on this dog to bring him back from the brink of death had exhausted and worried me. This dog and I had been on an incredible journey together. The thought of losing him was almost too much to bear.

I had lost so much, felt so much, loved so very much. The light faded, and the sunset glowed orange in the sky and still I stayed with Bailey. In a way I felt as if this was a testament to everything we'd been through. I didn't want to leave him and yet I knew I couldn't stay all night. Bailey had settled down on his bed, seemingly quite happy and unaware of his imminent departure, though I'd told him softly that he was leaving us the next day.

"You must promise to come back and visit all the time. I won't take no for an answer," I said finally, as the tears started to dry up. I wiped my face on my sleeve. "No one cares what I look like here, so I can do that," I hiccupped to Bailey, who through all the upset had just sat next to me, gazing into my face with his soft trusting black eyes. His body seemed to disappear into the darkness, and only his long nose and exquisite features stood out.

"If we hadn't found Mary and Ron so quickly, I would have kept you until you were fully restored to health, but something tells me you're going to be fine with them. They'll take good care of you, my darling boy."

At this point the dog yawned, which made me laugh.

"That's it, you tell me to shut up and go home to bed, and you're quite right. I'm an old lady and I should be tucked up in bed with a mug of cocoa rather than kneeling down in a kennel looking after you." I petted him as I spoke, and he never took his eyes off me.

My eyes filled with tears again, and my voice cracked with the love I felt for him. It was time to take my leave and get the rest I knew I needed. Turning to leave, I looked back into Bailey's soulful eyes.

"You've helped me in more ways than you can ever know, Bailey. I'm so honored to have met you. I couldn't have done it without you."

As if he understood, Bailey leaned forward and licked my nose. A simple, beautiful gesture. A doggie kiss I would cherish forever.

"Goodnight, beautiful boy. I'll be here to say goodbye when tomorrow comes."

I pulled the door shut, smiling at Bailey as he settled his head down on the bed.

The sky was streaked with the last flashes of orange, and night was falling. I stopped for a moment, listening to the contented cluck of the chickens and the occasional bark of a dog in one of the kennels. The sheep were bleating in a nearby field, and every now and then a horse would whinny. The heat had gone from the day, and I shivered in my T-shirt and trousers. It was time to get some rest and get tomorrow over with.

As I walked the few yards back up to my bungalow, I thought of that timeless bond between animal and human. How each is changed and healed by the other's loving presence and guidance. Bailey had been a perfect example of that interchange, the ancient call of companionship and togetherness between owner and dog. I would miss Bailey, but as I opened my front door and saw Harry and Gabby, ears pricked for my return, bound toward me, their tongues lolling out, racing in circles around my feet, I knew that this relationship wasn't ending; it was only changing and growing with my own dogs.

I bent down to give them both a cuddle.

"Mummy's home," I said.

Chapter 18

FOREVER FAMILY

"There they are. Their car has just turned into the parking lot," Diane said, turning to me and watching me in her usual knowing way.

I've never been able to hide any of my emotions, be it anger, fear, or joy. Every feeling I was capable of was written all over my face as if in a book. I would never have made a diplomat, or so Diane was fond of telling me.

We were both standing in the living room staring at the large screen showing the fuzzy CCTV images from around the sanctuary. I knew I looked subdued and restless. I'd tossed and turned all night, unable to sleep with the knowledge that Bailey would be leaving us today. I'd spent the morning pacing about, willing them to come and get the whole wretched ordeal over and done with. Then, after it was done, I would retreat into my chores and to-do list so I could work through my complicated feelings by myself. I'd always dealt with life that way; even as a child I was very self-contained. I never confronted my mum about how upset she often made me, even though she saw how grumpy and "difficult" I could be. She never tried to make me feel better, or ask me the source of my challenging behavior, and I would never have trusted her with my emotions. It simply never occurred to me to think I could go to her and tell her how I felt. Perhaps that's why I'd never learned to hide my outrage or my delight. Maybe I showed those feelings as a child because I was desperate for her to notice and soothe away my troubles. It never happened; any comfort I reaped was from loving my dad and helping him with the animals he brought home to look after. Peter and I were close too so I had an ally, but against the sheer force of my mother, or "grizzly bear" as we called her, this was scant comfort, but it was all I ever had.

"Here we go, then. At least they're a little early. It would've been worse to hang around waiting," I said, striding over to the screen to watch Mary and Ron get out of the car.

"I wonder if they'll bring the other greyhounds out? I hope so because it will be like being in a pack for Bailey, so he'll feel more comfortable, and . . ."

Before I finished my sentence, Mary opened up the back of the car, and Flash and Brandy jumped out.

"They're here. Come on, Barby, we can't put off this moment any longer," Di said, ushering me out of the living room.

Di hadn't really had much to do with Bailey, being primarily responsible for the cats, but she knew how much he meant to me. Everyone at the sanctuary had watched his progress with keen interest, either from near or afar, because it wasn't often we received an animal as much in peril as Bailey had been. It had been a huge source of pride for everyone that we had managed to save the dog and now give him a whole new chapter in his life.

As we walked over the yard, scattering the geese as we went, several volunteers said "Hello," "Sorry to hear he's going today," and "Chin up, Barby, it's the right decision."

Everyone knew this was a momentous day and were lending their support. I felt a lump in my throat and tried to swallow it down.

It won't do Bailey any good if you blub in front of him, I admonished myself as I paced. *Much better if you're bright and breezy and act as if you're happy to see him go off with his new owners. The more positive you are, the more it will help him settle. Come on, girl, you can do this . . .*

Ron and Mary had reached the gate by the time we got there. I held it open and led them through into the sanctuary.

"Hello, it's good to see you. Are you all ready to take him?" I asked as cheerily as I could manage.

By this time, Christine had joined us from the kennels. I turned to say hello and saw that she had Bailey on the leash with her. I wasn't expecting it all to happen so fast. I almost panicked. My heart started racing. Christine, seeing my disquiet, said: "Why don't you all go inside and sign the final forms so we can release Bailey to you, and I'll take him for a quick walk around the paddock."

I was so grateful for her stepping in. The proper protocol had vanished from my brain. I felt rather overwhelmed but managed to guide the couple into the house, and within minutes they'd signed the forms and we were ready. The point of goodbye had come so suddenly. The last few months rolled out in front of my mind's eye, and I felt a surge of gratitude for the journey both Bailey and myself had been on together.

"Can I please have a quick moment to say goodbye to him?" I asked Mary and Ron. "As you are his new owners officially now I thought I'd better ask you . . ."

Mary smiled, her kind face lighting up. "Of course, Barby. We're so delighted to have found him. Oh and by the way, if you don't mind, we've decided to change his name to Cookie. We feel we'd like to cut any links with his abusive past. I hope you understand. We were thinking a new name would be a fresh start for him. What do you think?"

Mary looked at me as if she was wary of what I'd say next. She looked almost nervous about my reply, as if I would ever try to tell her what she could do with her own dog.

"I think that's a brilliant idea," I replied straight away, beaming. "He is your dog now, and perhaps you are right. It's time to look to the future and to forget the past, though you'll forgive me if I remember him as Bailey."

Mary breathed a sigh of relief. "Thank you, Barby, I was so worried you would be upset by me saying that."

Ron added: "Thank you for doing such a wonderful job with him. He's a truly lovely dog."

I felt the tears rise up again. I had to get this done or I would be an absolute mess, and unable to say goodbye to the greyhound in the way that I wanted.

There was a slight pause as all three of us stood there. I laughed. "Come on, I'll lead the way."

We went back outside just as Christine came into view with Bailey trotting beside her. Behind them, the morning sunshine saturated the land in soft yellow light. The hills and valleys behind them seemed an endless ocean of green: green grass, green trees, leafy foliage everywhere. It was a bucolic sight and, not for the first time, I sent a fervent prayer of thanks for allowing us all to live and work in this beautiful place.

As we passed the kennels, the dogs started barking as if on cue.

"Those are the ones that won't be leaving yet. It's no wonder they bark, poor things," Christine said as if to herself.

I cut into her train of thought. I had to say my piece to Bailey or I was going to dissolve into tears. I've always hated goodbyes. I've said goodbyes to so many animals over the years, and in almost every case I've welled up. I've also said goodbye to so many people in my life, notably my brother Peter and my beloved father, of course. By my age, saying goodbye was becoming an occupational hazard. I just hoped that one day I would get used to it. That day certainly wouldn't be today.

"I'd like to have a minute with Bailey, please," I said gruffly, reaching for his leash. I walked him a few paces back where he'd just walked and knelt down with him, sneaking a biscuit out of my pocket, which he crunched on delightedly.

"I'm only going to say a few words to you, because we had our proper goodbye last night," I started, stopping to let the wave of emotion break over me. I cleared my throat, willing myself to go on.

"You have been the most marvelous dog, the most wonderful boy, and I will miss you very, very much. I know you will be happy with your new doggie siblings and your new owners, but please don't ever forget us here.

"I was honored to care for you. You showed such bravery, such trust. You taught me so much about myself, things that even at the age of seventy-three I still didn't know. I will never forget you, my darling, but it's time for you to go. Shall we walk to the gate together?"

Bailey looked up at me. His black fur shone in the sunlight. His eyes were liquid happiness. He stood there, graceful and serene and my heart almost burst with love for him.

"Let's go then, boy," was all I said as I led him over to the others. By now both Dan and Fran were there too, chatting with the couple and glancing over as I said my farewell to this beautiful creature.

"He's all yours," I said smiling, the first tears rolling down my cheeks. I didn't bother to hide them anymore. How could I? It was love that was making me cry, which is the noblest emotion and one I could never, ever be ashamed of.

I handed the leash to Mary, and she looked at me as if she understood everything I was feeling. She nodded and took the leash, leaving my hand empty and weightless.

"Shall we go home?" Ron asked Bailey and the other two dogs, then all three of them walked off with the couple.

We stood there watching them go. Bailey didn't turn back. He looked for all the world like he'd always been with his forever family. He had gone from our lives.

"Sorry, I have to leave you, it's all too much," I said and almost ran inside. Once in the safety of my bedroom, I let out my grief and howled there on the bed, my shoulders shaking as wave after wave of sorrow hit me like rolling breakers.

Gabby and Harry soon joined me, jumping up on the bed and sitting on either side of me, Gabby attempting to lick the tears off my face.

"You daft dog. You always know how to cheer me up," I giggled, pulling her into my arms for a cuddle. I breathed in her warm, clean doggie smell. Gabby turned her head to mine, her big brown eyes staring at me as if she understood every word.

"Bailey wasn't the only clever dog, was he, my angel?" I said, Gabby taking this as her cue to shower me in yet more kisses. "Nor the only gorgeous one in the world. We loved him, but he's had to leave us, but we'll be okay, won't we? Yes, we will. We'll be together, looking after each other . . ." I snuggled my face in Gabby's soft fur for a moment, and like magic my sadness started to lift. I sat there for a while. I could feel the constant, steady pace of Gabby's heartbeat, and it soothed me. I wiped my eyes, suddenly realizing I couldn't sit here all day crying like a baby. I had the Summer Bazaar to organize, and we had some new cats coming in today after a couple who were splitting up rang us in great distress as neither could take the pets into their new, separate rental accommodations. We had stalls to organize and raffle prizes to beg from the local businesses and transport to organize for the event. We had gulls to feed, hamsters to check over, forty-eight rabbits and their claws to trim alongside all the usual cleaning, clearing, feeding, nursing, and caring jobs we needed to do in the menagerie here twice a day, every day. There was no time for sorrow.

The moment had passed. Bailey had gone to a new home, and I had new animals to welcome into the Barby Keel Animal Sanctuary. It was just another day, already filled to the brim with the anguish and love that were ever-present here in this remarkable place.

Chapter 19

COMMUNITY SPIRIT

"Barby, Barby . . . it's happened again . . ." Di buzzed me on the walkie-talkie. I was out in the back garden, potting up plants to sell at the Summer Bazaar, which was only days away. It was only 10 a.m., but already the hot summer sunshine was burning the back of my neck.

"What is it, dear?" I asked, half an eye on the pot I was filling with compost.

"That was the police, Barby. The shop's been burgled again," Di answered, her voice urgent. "Come inside now . . ."

I didn't need telling twice. I threw down my trowel, and ran inside still wearing my wellies, which I would never normally do. I have a rule for the house that everyone takes off their outdoor shoes before coming in, a rule which is generally completely ignored.

"What happened?" I asked, reaching the living room, Gabby on my heels. She had been in the greenhouse with me, lying on an old blanket I kept in there for her to use. Like my shadow, she followed me straight inside.

Di and Dan were talking together. They both looked up at me as I came in.

"Now, sit down, Barby, this won't be easy to hear," Dan said, sensibly.

I took his advice. "Tell me everything," I said, looking him straight in the eyes. I knew that sometimes they shielded me from the worst information in order to protect me, but this time I wanted to know the details. Our shop was our financial lifeblood, and our dear friends worked there. I didn't want to be spared the truth.

"One of the volunteers, I don't know who, before you ask, arrived early to open up the shop and, instead, found the back door opened and the shop ransacked," Di said, breathlessly.

"Go on," was all I could say. My heart was pounding.

"It looks like the thieves broke in the day before and hid in the upstairs flat."

"But that's where we store the raffle prizes," I cut in.

"Yes, Barby, they took everything—*everything* that had been donated for the Summer Bazaar raffle. The police said they took all the whisky, gin, the boxes of toys, literally everything we'd begged, borrowed, and been given."

We all looked at each other.

"Go on," I said, feeling a combination of despair and pure rage.

Di said, "From the shop downstairs they'd taken all the money from that week, more than £850 in total."

"Plus they took a microwave and some men's clothing," added Dan. I looked back and forth between Dan and Di's faces. They both registered the same shock I was feeling.

"That money also included sponsorship money raised by one of our volunteers," I said. "What bastards, what complete and utter bastards."

"Yes," said Di simply. "But it's more than just a burglary," she added. "It throws the whole Summer Bazaar into jeopardy. How can we have our raffle, our main event, without any prizes?" She looked at me blankly. The full horror of what this might mean hit home.

"Oh God." I suddenly felt sick.

I took these robberies personally, getting very upset and angry at the utter callousness of people who were depriving my animals of that much-needed income, and now they'd possibly sunk our bazaar. The main fund-raising day of the year, and everything that had been donated by kind sponsors and friends locally was gone.

"How can we get prizes at such short notice?" I whispered. "The bazaar is two days away. What are we going to do?"

"Calm down, Barby," soothed Dan. "We can still have the bazaar—we just have to get on the phone and tell people what has happened. They'll rally round, you'll see."

I looked up at him. "Well, I don't know, I really don't. It's a lot to ask of people. I'm sorry but I don't share your optimism."

Dan shrugged. "You'll see . . ." was all he said. "I'm off to clean out the pigs. Let me know if there's anything I can do to help." His voice faded as he strode off.

My hand reached for the phone. Should I ring the *Bexhill Observer* and tell them the bazaar was canceled this year? Or would that mean those robbers had won? I didn't have time to ponder over it. If we were going to cancel, then it had to be now, as the event was so close. Then, from deep inside, I felt my old fearlessness come back.

I'll show those burglars . . . I thought to myself . . . *we'll put on the best bazaar this sanctuary has ever seen* . . . I didn't waste another moment.

That day I spent with my ear glued to the telephone receiver, cajoling, wheedling, calling on kindnesses again and again. I explained to each supporter what had happened, each local business, each pillar of our community. Time and time again, I witnessed how extraordinarily selfless people can be in a time of crisis.

Donations flooded in. By the end of that day, I had perhaps a hundred or more new prizes, ranging from expensive sets of toys to free trips out to local attractions. We had a bumper crop of rewards for our loyal visitors. I felt exhausted, but overwhelmed with the kindness and generosity we had been shown. Nonetheless, I couldn't shake the fear that something else might go wrong.

The next morning, I was fizzing with anxiety. We had one more day to go until we opened the doors, so I rang the *Bexhill Observer* and gave them one hell of a story for the week's paper, and virtually demanded that they send a photographer to show the people who had robbed us that we were thriving, despite their best efforts. I told the newspaper all the facts— including the point that my vet bills were £4,000 a month, and as the number of animals here increased each day, it was now costing us roughly £6,000 a month just to keep the sanctuary running. It made their crime seem all the more petty and calculating. Those people were literally taking food from our animals' mouths. Well, I wasn't going to take that lying down!

The day of the bazaar dawned bright, with a clear blue sky that promised yet more sunshine. All my volunteers had promised to be here to support the sanctuary in its time of need. Yet again I was left reeling by the kindness of those who loved animals. It was an antidote to the shocking events at the shop this year. I was still calling round to get any last-minute donations, and as I did so, I watched my workers buzz around the site like worker bees. Harry was going this way and that way with a wheelbarrow stacked up with prizes, with plants to put out for sale, and various things like more chairs to seat elderly visitors. Christine was marching to and fro carrying the hanging baskets she always made up so beautifully to decorate the sanctuary, and to sell of course. Dan was rushing around, frowning as he raced from one end of the sanctuary to the other, trying to get all the animals fed and watered, their bedding clean, and their coats brushed if need be, before the gates were opened at midday.

When I finally realized I couldn't call another person due to sheer exhaustion, I went to the kitchen, Gabby at my heels, and made a cuppa for myself and Diane. I knew she'd have been up since dawn, making the cattery orderly and making sure each animal was well cared for and happy before the arrival of the crowds. We always had dozens of people who came specifically to look for a pet to rehome, and so it was one of Di and Brenda's busiest days of the year.

I made my way out into the sunlight. It was a warm day with a slight breeze. Absolutely perfect for the event. I silently

thanked God as I walked, not just for the fact that no one was
hurt in the robbery, but also for each and every person and
animal who called this place home. My gratitude soared as
high as the white puffs of cloud that hovered overhead, providing moments of welcome shade.

The stalls on the left of the entrance were being set up with
goods and games to tempt our visitors in a long row of wooden
houses built specially for the occasion. Diane was arranging
the raffle prizes in one of the huts that lined the southern side
of the sanctuary site where the main part of the bazaar took
place. Christine was there as well, arranging her flower baskets
to sell, and various volunteers were still racing here and there
with wheelbarrows of clean straw and animal feed, making
sure that all the animals were ready to receive our guests, even
though it was almost 12 p.m.

As the time to open the bazaar arrived, we were finally
ready to unlock the gate, which had been closed for the morning so that we could prepare. Outside there was a long queue
of people snaking back along the drive.

I signaled to Christine to unfasten the gate, and as it swung
open a familiar set of shapes appeared as if from nowhere. I
blinked, wondering if my eyes were playing tricks on me.

They weren't.

Slowly but surely the figures came toward me. Two people
and three greyhounds, happily walking in through the entrance. Mary spotted me standing there, frozen to the spot.

"We thought we'd bring you a special visitor," she called.
I beamed at her. I couldn't speak, I was so thrilled and so
struck by how healthy, how wonderful Bailey now looked.

"We took him straight to our vet, and we carried on with the feeding program that you started here. He's always hungry, bless him, and I expect he always will be, but apart from that, he's a super dog and we love him dearly."

I could have clapped with happiness. I walked over to Bailey, renamed Cookie, and he greeted me with his tail wagging. He clearly remembered me. He licked my hand and stood still, waiting for me to stroke his lean body. It was a sun-drenched moment of pure happiness.

"Oh, Cookie, you are a sight for sore eyes. How good of you to bring him here, thank you so much," I said, looking back up at Mary and Ron. I was almost at a loss for words, which doesn't happen often.

"It's lovely to be back here. If you don't mind, we'll have a wander round. We never had the chance to explore the animals properly while we were here to see Cookie, so we've been looking forward to today," Ron said, looking round at the bustle of activity.

I stood there like a person suspended in time. Around me people came and went, guests, visitors, and workers. Everyone looked happy, the sun was shining, and it looked like people were already ordering cream teas and buying the many varieties of plants we sold. The tills were filling up already, but I was barely aware of all this as I watched Cookie walk off with his forever family, feeling that damned lump in my throat that appeared every time this special dog was in my thoughts.

The dog had touched so many lives and hearts at the shelter, yet it was the best possible outcome for the greyhound who now had two humans to love him back to full health, as well as two companion dogs to play with. Cookie sniffed the couple's outstretched hands and took the treats they both offered him. His tail wagged as he ate.

Just then Christine sidled up behind me. "What a lovely surprise, eh, Barby? Now you're not going to disgrace yourself and start wailing right here while we're surrounded by happiness, are you?" she said, nudging me with her elbow.

"I will if I want to," I replied truculently.

Christine burst into peals of laughter. "Oh Barby, I've never met anyone like you. You really are a funny old bird, but we love you." And with that she grabbed me in a hug that took my breath away.

I had to rehome animals every day, and it never got any easier, even though I'd been doing it for thirty-eight years. Cookie was a special case, though, and a special dog. It felt like my fate and that of Cookie were intertwined from the moment he arrived, staggering and collapsing onto the rain-sodden ground. Cookie, or Bailey, had fought back, and so had I, and, with the sweet promise of summer, I felt a renewed sense of optimism.

"Barby, we need you over at the bingo stand, there's a mix-up with the prizes," Harry called from one of the wooden huts.

"I'm coming, dearest," I said, turning round, ready to do whatever was needed of me to keep this extraordinary animal shelter going, whatever the cost. As I walked, my view was of the south end of the site, the bungalow to my left, the stalls and raffle behind me, the kennels almost straight ahead. Behind the kennels I could just see the paddock where we had three new horses brought in only a few days before.

I said a silent prayer of thanks to my friend Dorothy, or the Butterfly Lady as I called her. It was Dorothy, who had given the sanctuary the £10,000 deposit to buy the paddock only a few years earlier. I called it my Dream Field, as I'd wanted to buy the field next to our site for a long time before her generous donation. My friend was now housebound, and so, in honor of her love of nature and her altruism, one of the staff would pick her up from her home and drive her to the top of the field so she could see the animals without getting out. I knew she, like so many others, would be here today, enjoying the unique atmosphere that was this place, a place so utterly devoted to the care of abandoned creatures.

I stood for a moment gazing at the paddock, the horses munching on straw, their tails flicking the flies away, and silently gave thanks for all the kindnesses and blessings I'd received over the years.

"Come on, Barby, no time to dawdle!" Di said, grinning as she hurried me over to the bingo and the many guests who were wanting to greet me, to say hello, to reminisce over animals we'd known, or share their stories of successful rehomings. I smiled and bustled over to help Harry. After all, I am Barby Keel, the face of the Barby Keel Animal Sanctuary, and it was all just in a day's work.

"Hello, Harry, how can I help?" I asked, smiling broadly.

Epilogue

Every day something new, something unexpected, happens here at the Barby Keel Animal Sanctuary, the place I and five hundred animal residents now call home.

Today I am out on the land with a wonderful woman who does reiki on the animals, a kind of healing energy medicine that involves her touching the creature in need and channeling healing to them. I have no idea how or why it works but, as I stand back, I feel a strange sense of peace.

The healer, called Mandy, is crouched over one of our donkeys, a white and gray fellow who suffers from nerves and is generally twitchy and not happy being handled by people. He was abandoned in a field for a long time, and perhaps that is why he still finds contact unsettling. Yet the donkey is lying on the grass, his head in Mandy's hands as she bends over him, in complete concentration and stillness.

I am standing a few feet away at the end of the field, watching Mandy hold his right front leg with one hand and his head with the other. It is a moment of pure peace, and made possible by the loyal and unending support of everyone who donates money, time, and effort to this special place. Those people, who hold jumble sales and coffee mornings or donate animal food to our bins in various local supermarkets, are all heroes in my eyes. Everyone who works here as part of my motley crew, who contributes to our open days, who leaves us money in their will, or who makes large donations during the year, all these people are doing something wonderful.

Indeed, you, the reader, are directly contributing to the well-being of our animals by buying this book, and I am eternally grateful.

It is sometimes a thankless task running a place like this. We try to take every animal that is offered to us either by distraught, caring, loving owners who are forced by circumstance to give up their pets, or by those who neglect or mistreat their animals and no longer want them. We make no moral judgment outwardly because we know this might mean that someone doesn't bring their animal to us to be rescued, and instead might dump them elsewhere to avoid any possible consequences.

We take every animal we can, and I have always vowed never to destroy an animal that has a chance to live in peace and happiness with us.

Every day my work goes on: raising money, caring for strays, overseeing the charity, and giving homes and love to our feathered and furry friends. It can be very hard work, but when an animal like Bailey shows up, then I am sharply reminded of my task here. All the troubles, pressures, and issues fade away and my real work begins. Bailey gave me so much that I can never repay. He got me through another grueling bout of cancer and the weeks of radiation therapy, and I like to think I gave him the best I could in return. He is happy now, and during the long winter nights that followed his re-homing, I thought about him a lot, musing on the extraordinary strength and serenity he showed, and how through it all he just wanted someone to love him. I loved him, and so did many of my staff. He found comfort and care here with us, and I couldn't have asked for more from the tireless workers who surround me.

Sadly, many months later, my beloved Gabby died. One day she walked up the special stairs I'd had built by my bed so that she could easily get up, and she suddenly died in my arms. Grief is the consequence of having experienced pure love, and it is a price we all have to pay, whether with our adored pets or beloved friends and family. At least I got to hold her, to feel the warmth slowly leave her soft little body. I shut her eyes, looking for the last time at that deep honey gaze that was now fixed and absent. I wrapped a blanket around her and took her to Harry to let him sniff at her so that he could understand that she was gone from our lives. Otherwise he may have paced around endlessly looking for her, following the trail of her smell until it vanished completely, and the sight of that would've broken my heart all over again.

Saying goodbye is never easy. It doesn't get less painful. I knew I'd been privileged to have had Gabby in my life. She got me through the first bout of cancer, repaying every kindness, every ounce of patience for the hours I'd spent teaching her how to be a dog, teaching her to play, to go outside, to become her true doggie self, in spades. Every day I still miss her, just as every day I think of Bailey. The love never leaves me, it just expands and grows to encompass more and more animals as they come into this site on a daily basis.

Then another blow. My friend Christine succumbed to cancer in 2012. Words still cannot express the gap she has left in my life. She would have wanted me to carry on, to keep my doors, and heart, open for the next lot of abandoned, unloved, or simply unwanted animals. I have done that and I do it daily. Fran is still here, still battling his health condition, still a valued member of our team, though we tend to worry about him, and try to fuss over him, which he hates.

Life is a lottery. None of it really makes any sense. My brother died tragically young, yet here I am, still going strong despite two rounds of cancer. What I've learned, if anything, is that every day is a blessing as well as a challenge, but at the heart of each day is our prayer that no animal ever has to live in fear or pain while we are here.

Outside there can be harshness, unkindness, but in here, we show our animals, and hopefully our people, only love.

And I know I'll meet my Gabby, Peter, Dad, and Christine again on Rainbow Bridge. It is a place just this side of heaven where all the animals who have died will gather, happy but waiting until one day they spot my familiar face. Gabby's bright eyes will look into the distance, eager and intense. Her body will quiver with expectation. Then as she realizes that, yes, it is me, passing through the spirit lands, she will run, flying over the grass, tearing toward me. I will kneel in the grass and hold out my arms, waiting for the tumultuous embrace, the flash of fur and teeth, the bright amber-flecked eyes that will once again turn their trusting gaze to me. I wait for that day, but in the meantime I have work to do here in this world, on this land, at the Barby Keel Animal Sanctuary. If you would like more information about our sanctuary, please visit our website, http://barbykeel.btck.co.uk, which shows the dogs and cats who can be sponsored or rehomed, plus there is also the opportunity to donate to the sanctuary. Please support us.

These animals often have no one else to turn to.

If you enjoyed reading Bailey's story,
read this exclusive sample chapter of

Gabby: The Little Dog That Had to Learn to Bark

Available wherever print and e-books are sold!

Chapter 1

NEW ARRIVALS

The day dawned with bright summer light that glowed across the fields, the enclosures, and the landscape that surrounded us. Though we were only a short distance from the town center, it felt like we were a million miles away on mornings like this. Apart from the electricity transmission lines that sliced through the land, it was a rural idyll, and it felt like we were somehow apart from civilization. The backdrop to my life was the rolling, undulating Sussex countryside, and, of course, the sanctuary land that sheltered and housed animals of every description. I breathed in the smell of summer, that indefinable scent of flowers and grass, which mixed with the familiar sanctuary aroma of fresh straw, dry fur, and mud.

I yawned. The residents of the sanctuary had started their waking rituals at 4 A.M.: the roosters crowed as they struck their funny poses around the yard, the pigs grunted, the horses brayed in the back fields, the goats and sheep bleated for their breakfast. Then there were the dogs barking in the kennels, desperate for a walk, and the noise from the assorted ducks, geese, chickens, and seagulls that also resided here. Their squawks, clucks, honks, and screeches joined the cacophony, making me smile. It was just another day at the Animal Sanctuary.

"I'd better get up and make Dan some beans on toast. He'll be in for his breakfast soon," I muttered to myself as I hastily got dressed. My mind was already whirring from the list of jobs I had to get on with that morning. "I need to check with Diane about the cat who may be deaf. He's due to be rehomed soon, and so we must get him to the vet to check. The pigs need new straw, so I'll do that first. Those bundles are blimmin' heavy for an old lady like myself!" I chuckled.

I laughed because even though I was sixty-eight years old, I was fighting fit. Every morning at daybreak I'd get up, pull on a top and some trousers, and head out to clean out the animals, dragging huge sacks of goat or sheep feed, pulling a bale of hay onto my back or striding over the fields in search of a missing goat. I never felt my age. I'd spent my life working hard, and it didn't occur to me for a minute that I might retire one day. Why would I want to sit around with nothing to do? That would kill me faster than any hard labor, or so I thought.

I'd bought this land thirty-one years ago with a view to taking in a few unwanted or abandoned animals or strays. Within a few months of setting up in my leaky RV on the site, the trickle of strays had turned into a deluge, with the horses, goats, dogs, and donkeys all roaming free, as animals should be, on my land. All I had to contain them was a fence that ran around the perimeter of the site, which I'd sold my car as well as canceled my life insurance to help pay for. I figured that without children, I had no one to inherit anything anyway. That's how daft I've always been about animals—I'd do anything to help them.

"Are you doing my breakfast, Barby? Not a problem if not," smiled Dan, as he ambled in.

Dan always had a twinkle in his eye, always teasing me in his gentle way. He was our farm manager and took care of the larger beasts. He was one of my most trusted staff, a tall man in his early thirties with dark hair and glasses, quietly spoken and utterly capable, though I berated him often for his "laid-back" attitude. I am pretty feisty, as any of my volunteers would testify, but underneath it I'm also a worrier—and his calm approach to the dramas we encountered here on a daily basis drove me crazy at times. We would have badly treated animals being dumped here, six or seven unwanted cats arriving every day, animals always needing medical attention, sometimes urgently, and this all combined to make me feel overwhelmed at times. Dan, who had worked here for six years, would shrug his shoulders and get on with the task in hand, in his own way and in his own time. Probably because of our differences, we made a good team.

"There you go, here's your breakfast," I said, handing Dan a plate of steaming hot baked beans. "There's toast in the toaster. Now I'd better get on and look at those documents from yesterday before I go out . . ." I always made him his breakfast. It was part of our routine. He did all the big, dirty jobs on the site, so it was my small way of showing appreciation.

Wandering into the living room of my sprawling bungalow,

I spotted a pile of forms that I needed to attend to. Every time an animal such as a cat or dog is brought to the rescue center, the previous owners have to sign a form signing away any rights they have over their pet to the Animal Sanctuary. We have strict procedures in place to make sure that each animal is properly registered, given immediate medical attention if needed, and either spayed or neutered to prevent any more unwanted creatures coming into the world. Animals such as pigs, deer, sheep, cows, and goats are subject to a Defra Movement General Licence, which means that we have to follow government guidelines, whereas our forms for cats and dogs are more of a formality than an official requirement, but it gives us the confidence and assurance that the animals were being handed to us completely, and that after the seven-day cooling-off period, they become our legal responsibility.

It has to be this way. The number of people who ring up after a few months because they've changed their minds and want their pet back is astonishing. We feel the animals are best served by stability, care, and rehoming as quickly as possible into loving, permanent homes. It can be an emotional, and often extremely difficult, decision to give up a beloved pet, and we understand how traumatic it can be, for humans and animals alike, which is why we have processes in place to mitigate that stress for everyone. Animals need love, care, the right food, and exercise, and we know that circumstances change and this can become a burden. Pets develop behavioral problems, or fall ill and need expensive medical treatment, which forces families in poverty to say good-bye, but we also know that some people simply don't want their animal, or have grown tired of the expense and commitment.

We're always here to pick up the pieces and take in these unwanted pets, otherwise what would happen to them? God only knows. Yet, I always dread having to go through the paperwork!

Just as I sat down, a steaming cup of tea in my hand, shuffling that pile of documents, something caught my eye—a swift, sharp movement outside. I peered out through the sliding glass door that led out into a small sunroom beyond the living room. I blinked and was greeted by a blaze of color. Emerald green feathers resplendent in the sunshine, a tall azure neck, and a crest of shimmering feathers over the peacock's head. I stood for a moment, spellbound.

"Dan, Dan, are you there, dear?" He'd wolfed down his meal and had already left by the time I came out of the reverie this magnificent creature had sent me into. I clutched my walkie-talkie to my mouth. It was the simplest way of reaching my staff and volunteers across the four-acre site.

A man's voice spoke, crackling: "Barby, all okay?"

"Dan, would you please come back over to the house? I've got a surprise for you . . ." I almost laughed with delight.

The peacock was proudly strutting around my yard, forcing the chickens and geese that roamed free to scatter, clucking with indignation as they went. The magnificent bird, a glorious creature, was already looking very "at home" in the sanctuary.

Dan appeared from the direction of the farm animal enclosures that lay beyond my gaze. He stopped for a moment just to look. I watched him gaze at the peacock before he turned to come into the house. My place was a single-story bungalow with one "upstairs" room, which was used for storage, more of an attic than a proper room. Over the years, I'd added an annex that had housed my father until he died at the grand old age of ninety-six, and a sunroom for both myself and Dad. I had a covered area to the right of my front door, which was on the southern side, with shaded seating for our visitors during the summer months. Once inside, the front door opened into a short corridor that led to the kitchen, with my lounge on the left and my bedroom farther up the hallway. It wasn't a big place but it was just right for me. My living room was always rather full, with filing cabinets, a sofa and armchairs for volunteers to drink their break-time cuppas, and a huge glass-fronted cabinet filled to the brim with my darts trophies. Animals weren't my only passion. I'd played for darts teams for decades and had won many a shiny cup or shield, and they were a source of huge pride to me.

"Well, we've definitely got a new peacock!" Dan said as he marched into the living room.

"Do you reckon he's one of those that went astray?" I asked, referring to the fact that a wealthy couple had decided to give up their muster of peacocks two years previously after finding that, although they looked beautiful, they made a hell of a lot of noise.

"Well, we had three or four peacocks left with us by that couple, so perhaps so. This one may have run off and somehow survived scavenging until now," said Dan, rubbing his chin thoughtfully.

We both looked back at the incredible bird that had now dropped his crowning glory of feathers and was stalking off toward the cattery.

"He's a beauty, that's for sure," I murmured, "and I'm going to call him Peter. Peter the Peacock."

"Alright, Barby," Dan interjected. "I'm off to feed the pigs. They've been given the new straw, so you don't have to worry about that. They're already busy making it into their bed."

Pigs are amazing creatures. All you do is dump the straw in the middle of their pen, and they will create their own sleeping area, which they never foul, making them one of the cleanest animals there is.

"Okay Dan, thank you, dear," I replied, still lost in thought.

There was something magical about peacocks—and strangely, I felt a pull toward this one. Perhaps that's why I'd chosen to name him after my beloved brother, who died at the tragically early age of fifty-eight, twelve years ago, though it still felt like yesterday. He'd had leukemia. He had been too young to die, and here I still was, aged sixty-eight and still going strong. I missed him every single day. He was my older brother by two years, and the person I had been closest to in the world, apart from Dad. Life just wasn't fair sometimes. My brother hadn't been a particular fan of peacocks, so I had no idea why I named the creature after him—except the desire to remember and appreciate something so otherworldly. I've always been sentimental—about animals mostly—but when it came to my brother, there was no limit to my love, and it spilled out in ways like this.

My musing was broken by the phone ringing. I probably fielded twenty to thirty calls a day.

"Hello, can I help you?"

"Hello, I'm ringing on behalf of my relatives. They're very elderly and are having to go into a home. They have four dogs. The greyhound and gorgeous Lhasa Apso are being rehomed, but we still have two that we can't find places for. Could you please take them?"

I paused for a second. My mind flitted straight from Peter and the peacock to this new dilemma. That's how life worked here. We never had a second to think. I wasn't sure we had room in the kennels, but instantly I couldn't bear the thought of those poor dogs being left without anywhere to go.

"I'll speak to Fran, who helps look after the dogs, but I'm pretty sure we'll have them. What breeds are they?"

"Kenny is a Jack Russell, and Jessy is a Yorkshire terrier. We'd be so grateful if you could help us."

"We'll make room for them somehow, don't worry," I replied. "When can you bring them in?"

The arrangements were made, and as soon as the phone call had ended, I buzzed through to Fran, who was out feeding the horses. Fran was a stocky, fair-haired man who came in a couple of days a week and had only been working at the sanctuary for a few months. He confirmed that the kennels were full. At that point I had a brainstorm and dived for my book. This book was the heart of the sanctuary, as it contained all the phone numbers and names of anyone who had ever rung to ask about taking in cats or dogs. I leafed through it.

"Bingo!" I said out loud.

Reaching for the phone, I dialed the number.

"Hello, dear. Do you still want two terriers?" I didn't need to stand on ceremony, as the woman who wanted to rehome two dogs was an old pal of mine, Ivy.

The lady's response was an unequivocal yes!

"Well, I've got two coming in later today. I'll get them checked in, make sure they're both okay, and we could get them over to you this evening. Is that alright?"

The elderly woman on the other end was delighted. She had been a friend of the sanctuary, and of me, for many years, and so we didn't have to carry out the usual home visits before rehoming the dogs with her—I'd been round to her place many times. It looked like the fates had smiled on us. *Peter the Peacock, you must be a good luck charm*, I said to myself as the startlingly beautiful creature walked back across the yard in front of my window, looking for all the world as if he owned the place.

Later that day, after I'd spent a good deal of time outside helping Dan with the goats, a man and a woman arrived, bringing with them the two dogs—one was a ball of long straggly fur that looked like it had been bleached blond and left with dark roots, and the other was a sweet-looking brown and white short-haired thing with a small, almost pug-like face. They both looked alert and eager, smelling the ground as they walked, their tails wagging. They were both the dearest little things. The ball of fur was carrying a red rag doll in its mouth as he trotted along, seemingly oblivious to the big change that was about to happen, while the short-haired ter-rier walked straight up to me and gave me a friendly sniff.

I greeted them all in the yard, conscious that my hair was not the tidiest, nor my wellies very clean. The couple didn't seem to mind. They smiled warmly and thanked me for taking in the dogs.

"You're in luck," I beamed, "assuming they're both okay, they'll be rehomed tonight. They came in at exactly the right time."

Once the formalities were over and the couple had signed the dogs over to me and left the sanctuary, they were checked over in the "emergency" extra kennel we'd had built for moments like this. They seemed like friendly dogs, and apparently they both submitted to the checks with good grace. The Yorkshire terrier had been particularly lovely, and he kept licking my hand as I stroked him when he first arrived.

As a foster carer, I knew I couldn't get too attached to each new dog, however gorgeous they were. My job with these two was to prepare them to go straight over to my friend's, and I did just that. Many animals arrive in a state of fear or trauma, or are simply stressed to be in a new place with strange people. I treat them all with the same gentleness and understanding, knowing that it didn't serve anyone if I became too fond of them.

"Now, you're both lovely, but you've got a new home to go to, and one of my motley crew will run you down there just as soon as we're happy that you're both okay," I said to them.

While the checks were taking place at the kennels, I returned to my living room and scanned the forms that all previous owners have to fill out, which ran to six pages for dogs. The documents listed all the information we might need, from questions about the dog's behavior, to their previous home life, history, and ability to play and eat and whether they were comfortable around people. There seemed to be nothing that jumped out. Each dog had lived in the one place with the elderly couple who were now too poorly to look after them, and they were both in good condition. They'd obviously been treated well. Their fur was glossy, they had no obvious marks, scars, or issues that I'd been able to see upon first inspection, and they were both a good weight. Instinctively I knew we could safely rehome them.

Just as I finished reading, the walkie-talkie buzzed. I picked it up. By now I was tired, yet I tried to keep the weariness out of my voice. It was Dan. Apparently a member of the public had reported an abandoned horse to him. He was asking if there was space for another horse on the site.

"We always make room, dearest," I said. "Go ahead and see who owns it."

It was just another busy day at the shelter.

Connect with U s

Visit us online at
KensingtonBooks.com
to read more from your favorite authors, see books
by series, view reading group guides, and more.

for sneak peeks, chances to win books and prize packs,
and to share your thoughts with other readers.

facebook.com/kensingtonpublishing
twitter.com/kensingtonbooks

Tell us what you think!

To share your thoughts, submit a review,
or sign up for our eNewsletters, please visit:
KensingtonBooks.com/TellUs.